How to Haunt Your House

Halloween Craft Fun

SCARY PROJECTS THE WHOLE FAMILY CAN MAKE

SCHIFFER CRAFT

4880 Lower Valley Road • Atglen, PA 19310

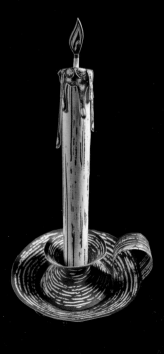

Published by Schiffer Publishing, Ltd.
4880 Lower Valley Road
Atglen, PA 19310
Phone: (610) 593-1777; Fax: (610) 593-2002
Email: Info@schifferbooks.com
Web: www.schifferbooks.com

Deadication

This book is dedicated to our three brave children . . . Michaela, Elijah, and Ryan. You each traveled down a dark and fearful path to find us. Both your lives and ours were changed forever. Through all the learning curves, up-and-down times, big changes and little moments, frustration and laughter, tears, and hugs . . . we all began rewriting our story as the *Mitchell Family.* Love heals wounds. Togetherness conquers fear. The spirits of our past help guide through our tomorrows. Please know that the jack-o'-lantern's light will always be lit so that you may know where home *truly is.*

Contents

Materials

These are some basic tools and materials needed for the projects in this book. Each project has specific requirements listed, but in general, these represent a handy crafter's toolbox.

1 Scissors *(for fabric and paper cutting)*

2 White Elmer's Glue bottle, glue sticks, Modge Podge, wood glue, spray glue *(for paper)*, Super Glue

3 Low-heat hot-glue gun *(make sure kids get instructions and can safely use, if needed)*

4 Yarn *(bright white and black)*

5 Copied patterns from book printed on regular copy paper *(or downloaded from website)*

6 Cardstock or similar heavy weight paper

7 Scotch tape, masking tape, gold Wasabi tape *(optional)*

8 Wooden tree rounds of various sizes & ½-inch sticks from yard

9 Wooden beads in various sizes with holes

10 Crepe paper rolls *(black, orange, white, greens, or gray)*

11 Paper plates & paper towels

12 Plastic wrap & tinfoil

13 Small bowl & sponge, rag

14 Clothespins

15 Paintbrush

16 Sanding block

17 Black form core boards *(black interior)*

18 Black illustration board or matte board

19 Picture frame hooks & removable wall hooks

20 Craft paints *(black, brown, red, metallic gold, oranges, greens, purple)*

21 Popsicle sticks, or flat craft wood sticks

22 Craft wire *(thin gauge)*

23 White pipe cleaners

24 Mini plastic skulls

25 Large buttons

26 Drill, 2-inch screw, 11/64-inch drill bit

27 Cheesecloth

28 Needlenose pliers or wire cutters, small detail screwdriver

29 Multiple widths and patterns of Halloween ribbons & string

30 Ruler

31 Wooden skewers *(small and large)* & wooden toothpicks *(with pointed ends)*

32 Multipurpose strong string

33 Clear rub-on wax

34 Coffee stirrers or juice box straws

35 Colored pencils

36 Cotton swabs

37 Utility knife and extra blades

38 Various sizes of photo matte frames *(optional)*

39 Pack of metallic photo frames *(optional)*

40 Tiny metal hinges *(optional)*

41 Quarter yard of red, faux velvet fabric

42 Decorative spiders

43 Small twigs and tree branch *(optional)*

Folded-Paper Spider's Web

Multi-size Decorations

YOU WILL NEED: Printed paper templates on regular copy paper for large and small spider-webs and spiders, scissors, glue stick, white paper plates, school glue, X-acto knife, bright white yarn, white card stock paper, tape, spray glue, removable wall hooks *(optional)*

T his is a fun exercise in folding paper with a nostalgic nod to a 1930s Halloween party. The spiderweb fans can be suspended from the ceiling or hung on a wall, and as a bonus, the webs glow under black light.

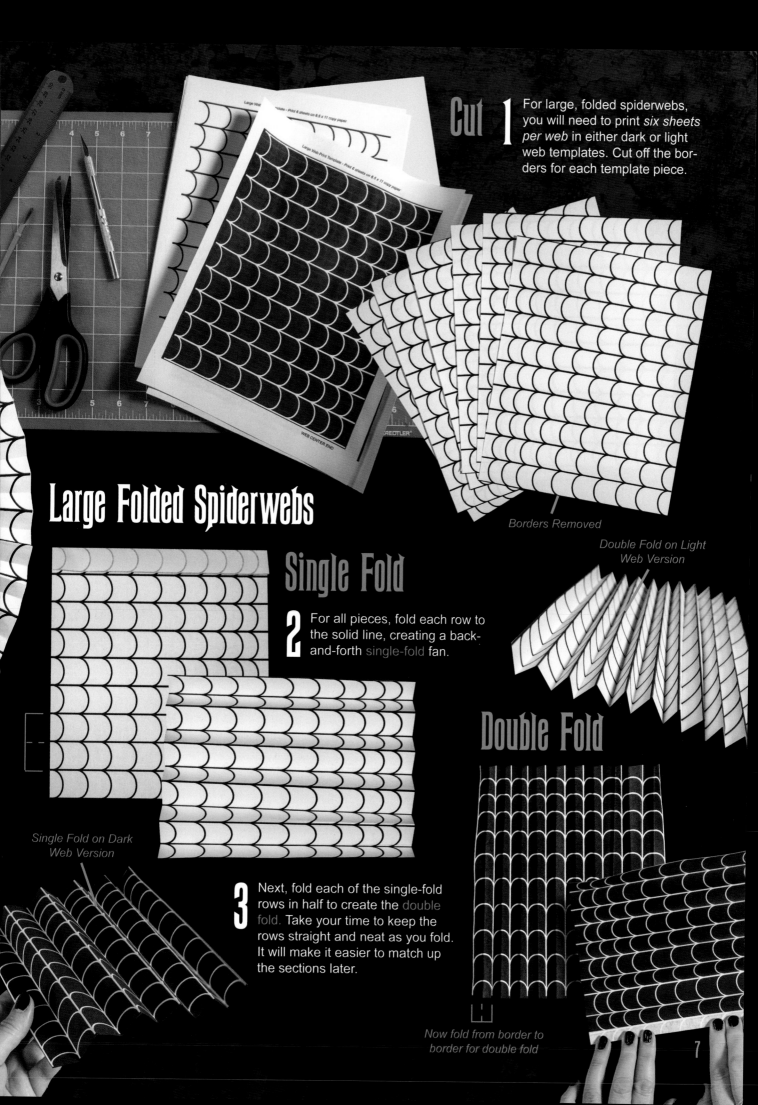

Cut

1 For large, folded spiderwebs, you will need to print *six sheets per web* in either dark or light web templates. Cut off the borders for each template piece.

Borders Removed

Large Folded Spiderwebs

Single Fold

2 For all pieces, fold each row to the solid line, creating a back-and-forth single-fold fan.

Single Fold on Dark Web Version

Double Fold on Light Web Version

Double Fold

3 Next, fold each of the single-fold rows in half to create the double fold. Take your time to keep the rows straight and neat as you fold. It will make it easier to match up the sections later.

Now fold from border to border for double fold

7

Assembling the Sections

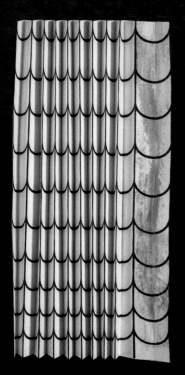
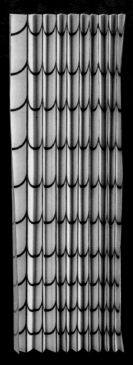

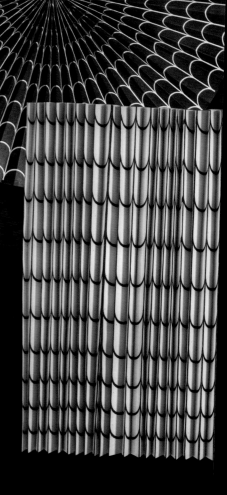

Paste Sections

4 Once you have all six sections folded, make sure they are all facing the same direction. There are *inside* and *outside* web ends. Use a glue stick to attach an end row to another fan section end row. Use the glue stick lid to flatten by firmly pressing the glued parts. Refold the glued row to match the folds before it. Continue the same steps until all six pieces are glued together in a row.

5 Take the first and last ends and glue those together with the print sides facing outward. With all six parts glued together, they will form a cylinder. Gather up the top web interior edge so that it forms a point. Slowly push this gathered end downward until it flattens out into a disk. Place a hand on each side of the fan disk and carefully turn it over.

Flatten Shape

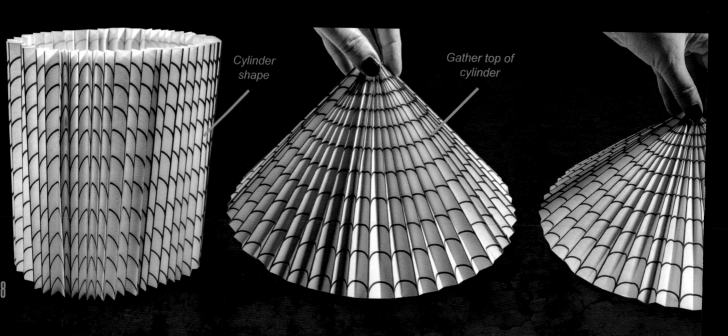

Cylinder shape

Gather top of cylinder

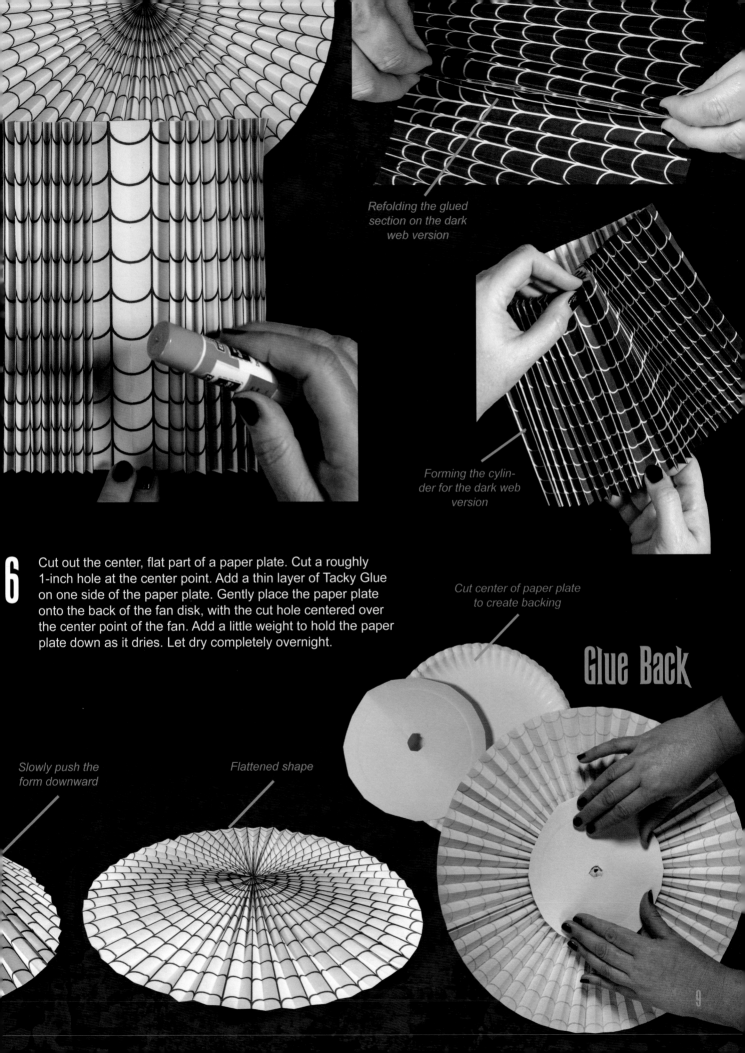

Refolding the glued section on the dark web version

Forming the cylinder for the dark web version

6 Cut out the center, flat part of a paper plate. Cut a roughly 1-inch hole at the center point. Add a thin layer of Tacky Glue on one side of the paper plate. Gently place the paper plate onto the back of the fan disk, with the cut hole centered over the center point of the fan. Add a little weight to hold the paper plate down as it dries. Let dry completely overnight.

Cut center of paper plate to create backing

Glue Back

Slowly push the form downward

Flattened shape

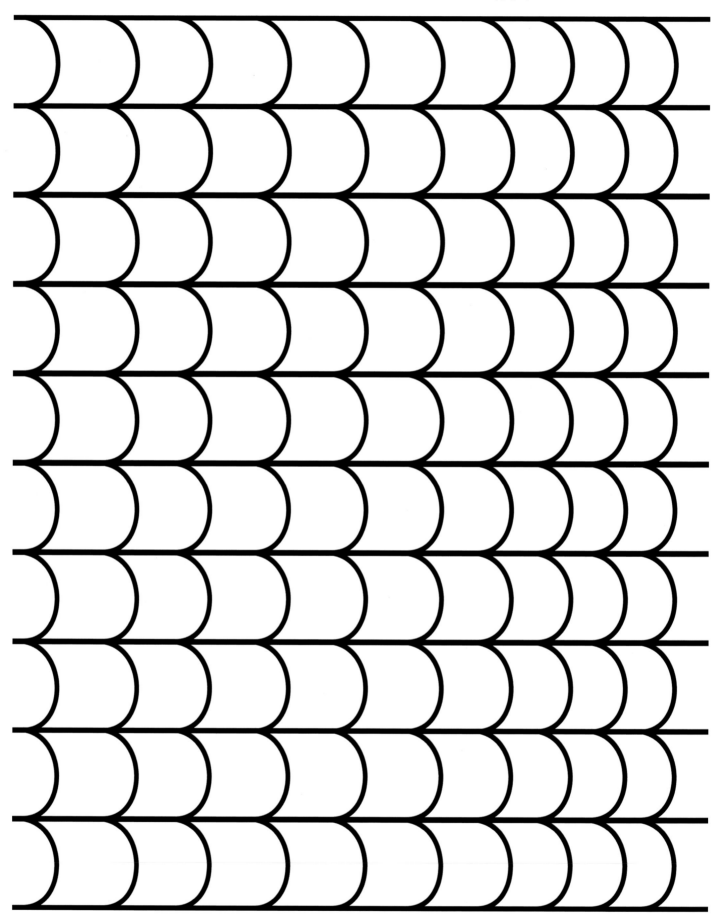

10   WEB OUTER EDGE

WEB CENTER EDGE

Large Web Print Template: *Print 6 sheets on 8.5 x 11 copy paper*

WEB OUTER EDGE

WEB CENTER EDGE

11

Small Folded Spiderwebs

Cut

1 The small folded spiderweb uses four panels from two template sheets. Cut down the centerline of the template to divide the two panels. Then cut off all the white borders from each panel.

2 Fold all the single folds at the horizontal template lines to create the single-fold fan shape.

3 The double fold will fold to the center of each of the previous folds. Once folded, squeeze stack tightly together, as shown.

Cut at centerline to get two pieces

Borders removed

Glue ends together

Paste

4 Glue the end rows of all template pieces together. Then glue the beginning and end rows together to form the cylinder, with printed side turned outward.

Squeeze all the folds tightly together

Single Fold

Double Fold

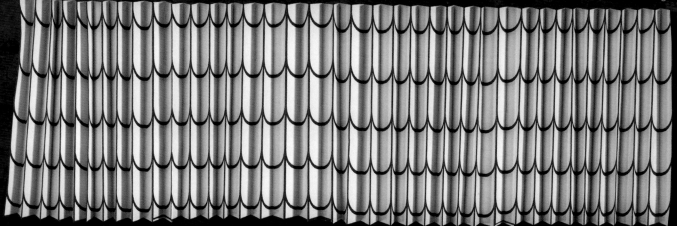

Flatten Shape

5 Gather up the web center edge and bring to a point. Slowly press the point downward until the shape flattens completely out to form a disk. Carefully turn the disk over to the backside.

6 Cut out the center of a paper plate. Cut a roughly 1-inch hole in the center. Use Tacky Glue to glue this onto the back of the disk. Add a bit of weight to hold the paper plate down as it dries. Let dry overnight.

Web center edge

Web outer edge

Glue Back

Add weight to keep in place as it dries

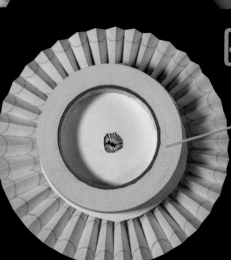

Small dark web version

Small Web Print Template: *Print 1 sheet on 8.5 x 11 copy paper*

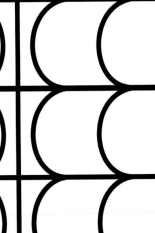

CUT CENTER LINE

WEB OUTER EDGE   WEB CENTER EDGE   WEB CENTER EDGE   WEB OUTER EDGE

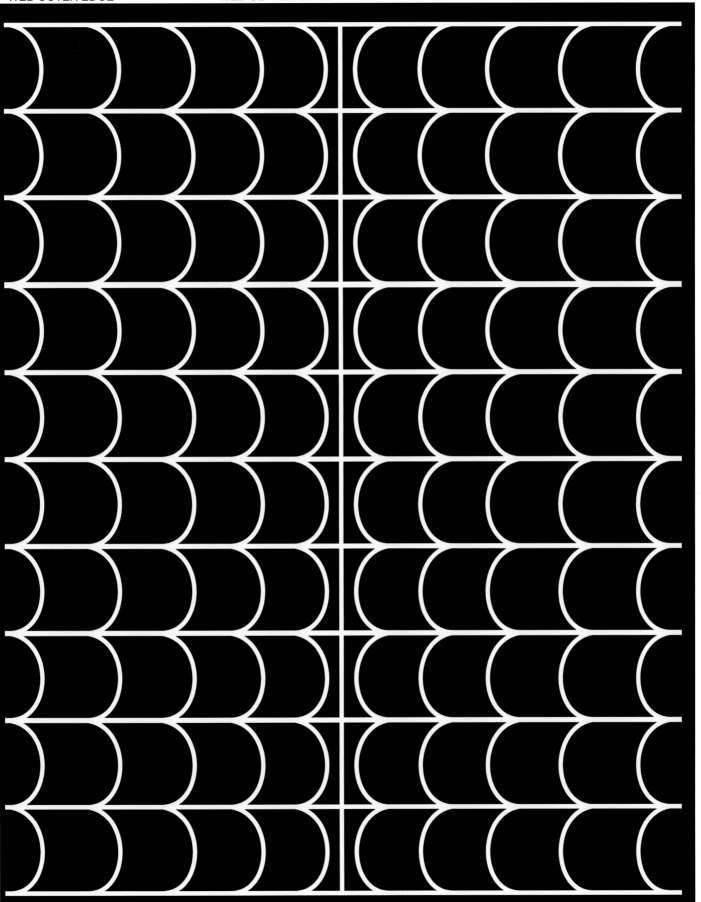

CUT CENTER LINE

Making the Spider

1 Print out the spider design on regular copy paper. Fold in half so the printed design is on the outside. This will create a front and backside print of the spider.

2 Make a cut between both back legs of the spider. Cut a V shape out just below the spider abdomen, as shown. This space will be for the string.

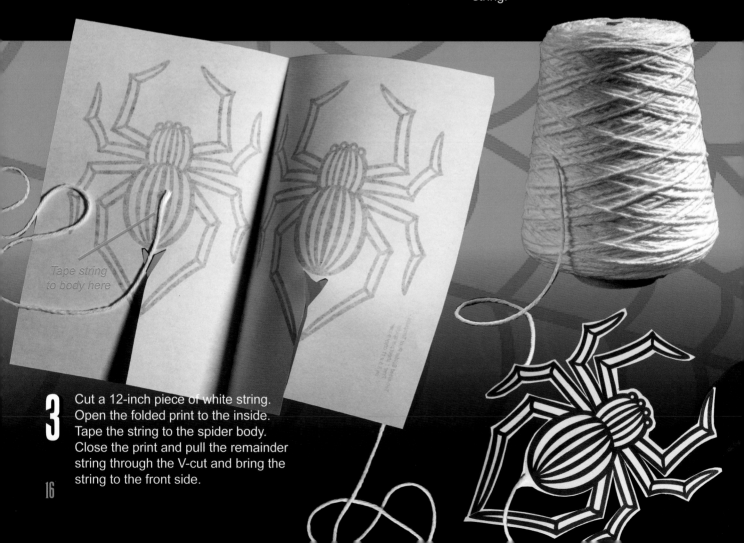

3 Cut a 12-inch piece of white string. Open the folded print to the inside. Tape the string to the spider body. Close the print and pull the remainder string through the V-cut and bring the string to the front side.

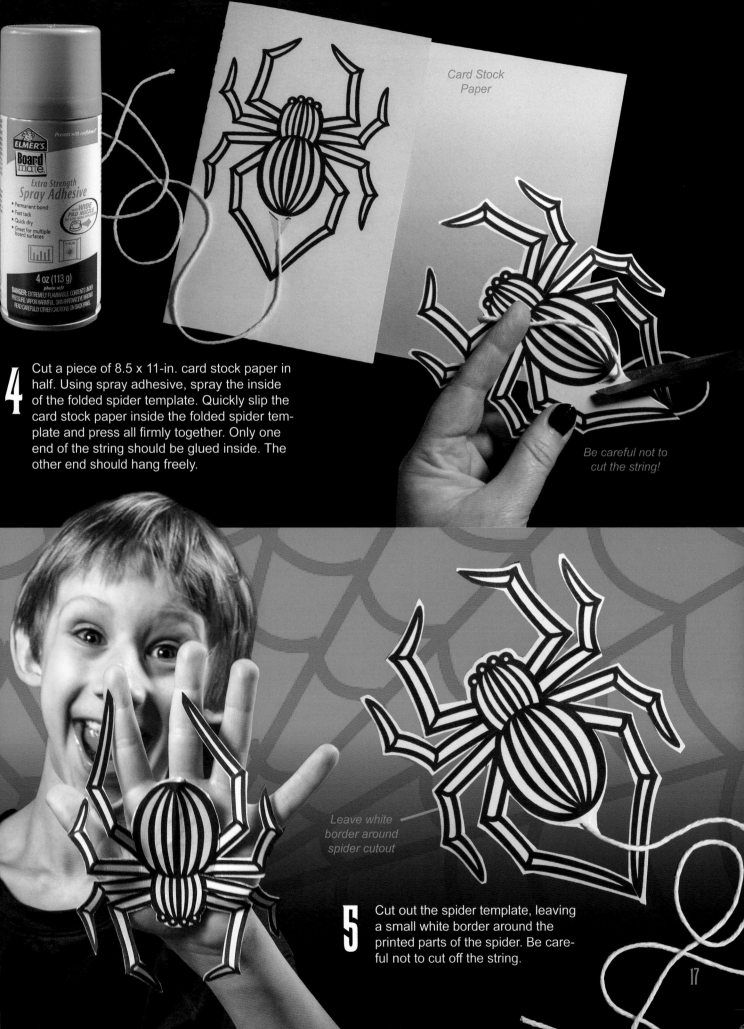

4 Cut a piece of 8.5 x 11-in. card stock paper in half. Using spray adhesive, spray the inside of the folded spider template. Quickly slip the card stock paper inside the folded spider template and press all firmly together. Only one end of the string should be glued inside. The other end should hang freely.

Card Stock
Paper

*Be careful not to
cut the string!*

*Leave white
border around
spider cutout*

5 Cut out the spider template, leaving a small white border around the printed parts of the spider. Be careful not to cut off the string.

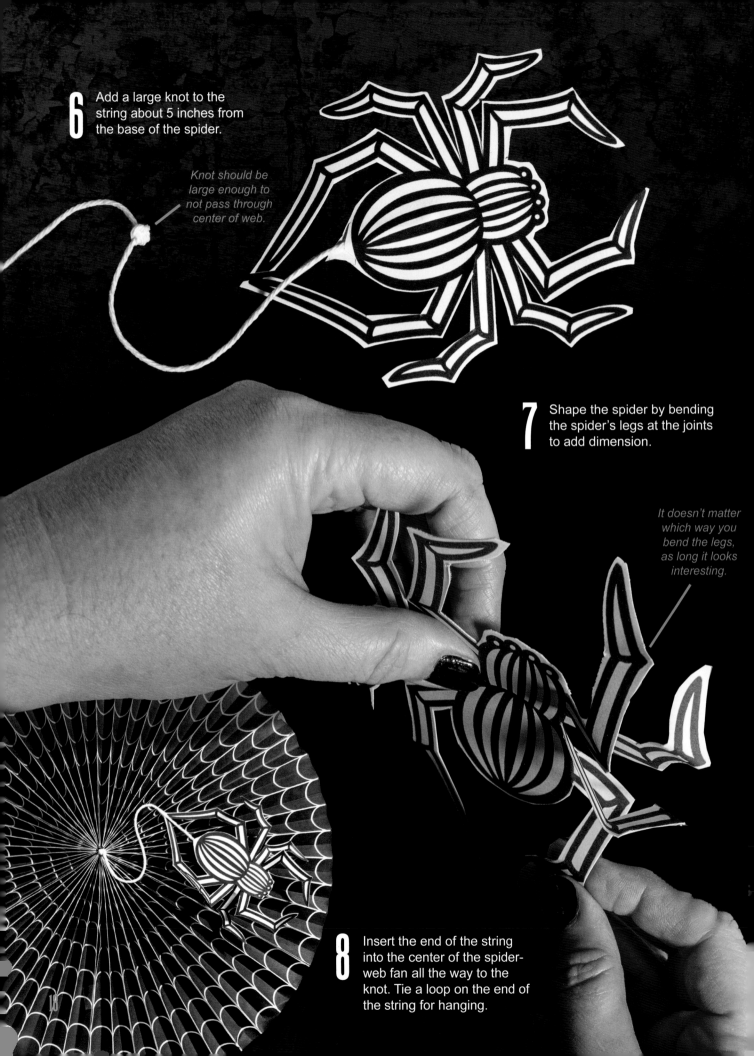

6 Add a large knot to the string about 5 inches from the base of the spider.

Knot should be large enough to not pass through center of web.

7 Shape the spider by bending the spider's legs at the joints to add dimension.

It doesn't matter which way you bend the legs, as long it looks interesting.

8 Insert the end of the string into the center of the spider-web fan all the way to the knot. Tie a loop on the end of the string for hanging.

Two-Sided Spider Print Template:
Print 1 sheet per spider
on 8.5 x 11 copy paper

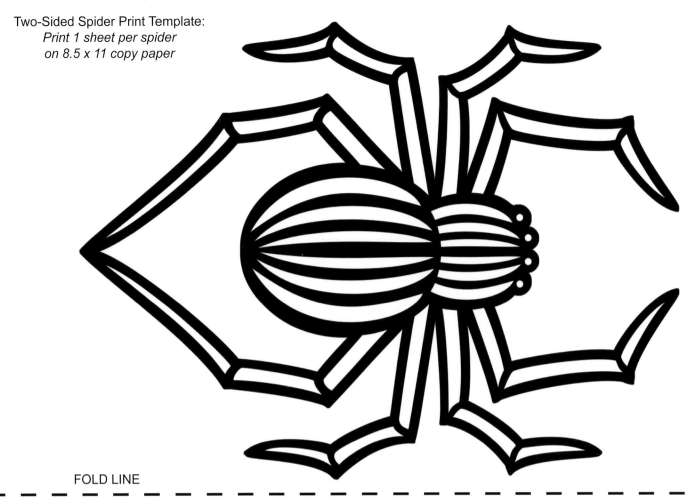

FOLD LINE

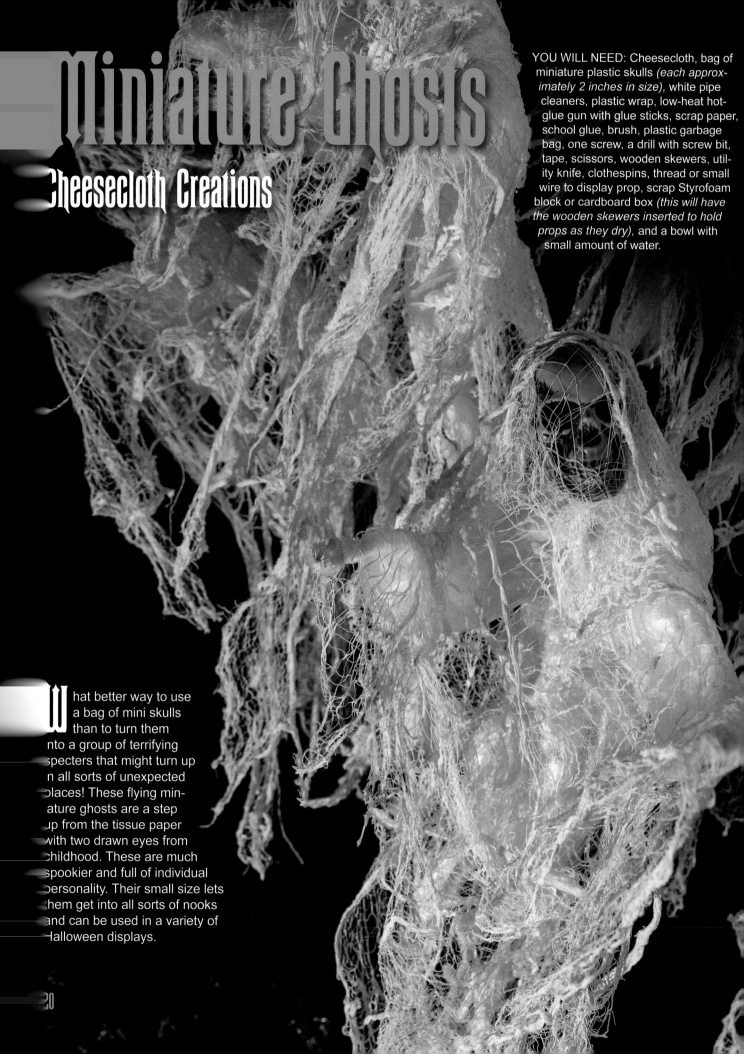

Miniature Ghosts

Cheesecloth Creations

YOU WILL NEED: Cheesecloth, bag of miniature plastic skulls *(each approximately 2 inches in size)*, white pipe cleaners, plastic wrap, low-heat hot-glue gun with glue sticks, scrap paper, school glue, brush, plastic garbage bag, one screw, a drill with screw bit, tape, scissors, wooden skewers, utility knife, clothespins, thread or small wire to display prop, scrap Styrofoam block or cardboard box *(this will have the wooden skewers inserted to hold props as they dry)*, and a bowl with small amount of water.

What better way to use a bag of mini skulls than to turn them into a group of terrifying specters that might turn up in all sorts of unexpected places! These flying miniature ghosts are a step up from the tissue paper with two drawn eyes from childhood. These are much spookier and full of individual personality. Their small size lets them get into all sorts of nooks and can be used in a variety of Halloween displays.

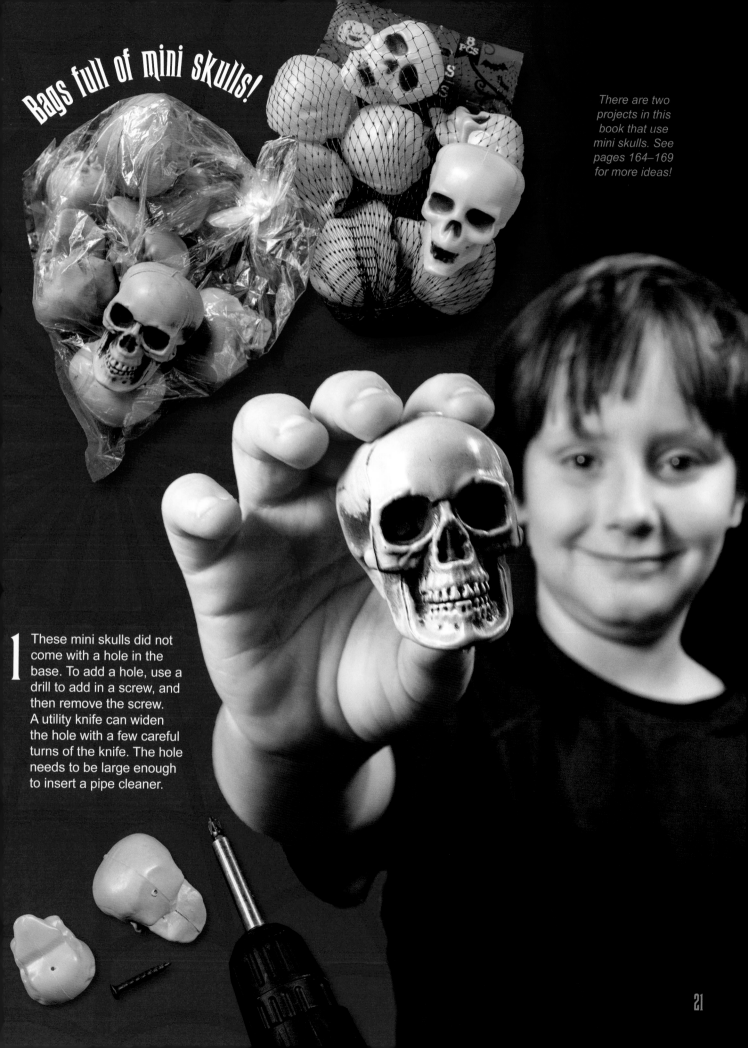

Bags full of mini skulls!

There are two projects in this book that use mini skulls. See pages 164–169 for more ideas!

1 These mini skulls did not come with a hole in the base. To add a hole, use a drill to add in a screw, and then remove the screw. A utility knife can widen the hole with a few careful turns of the knife. The hole needs to be large enough to insert a pipe cleaner.

2 Twist two white pipe cleaners tightly together for a stronger pipe cleaner. Create three of these double-wire pipe cleaners per skull.

3 Insert one of the double wires into the hole at the bottom of the skull. This will be the body.

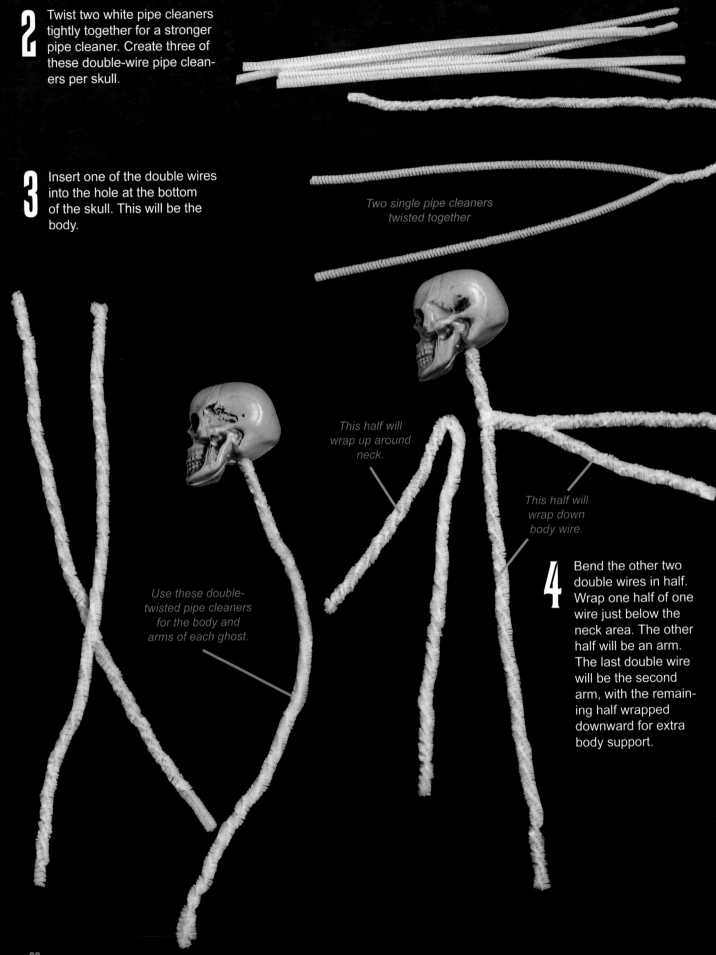

Two single pipe cleaners twisted together

This half will wrap up around neck.

This half will wrap down body wire.

Use these double-twisted pipe cleaners for the body and arms of each ghost.

4 Bend the other two double wires in half. Wrap one half of one wire just below the neck area. The other half will be an arm. The last double wire will be the second arm, with the remaining half wrapped downward for extra body support.

Bend ends over
to form hands

5 Bend the ends of each arm into a small loop for a hand shape and make a bend for each elbow on both arms. Add a small amount of low-heat hot glue to keep the wire and skull from coming apart.

Elbow

A not-too-scary-sized ghost!

To keep the head and neck from coming apart, add a bit of low-heat hot glue.

Now the head can be posed as needed.

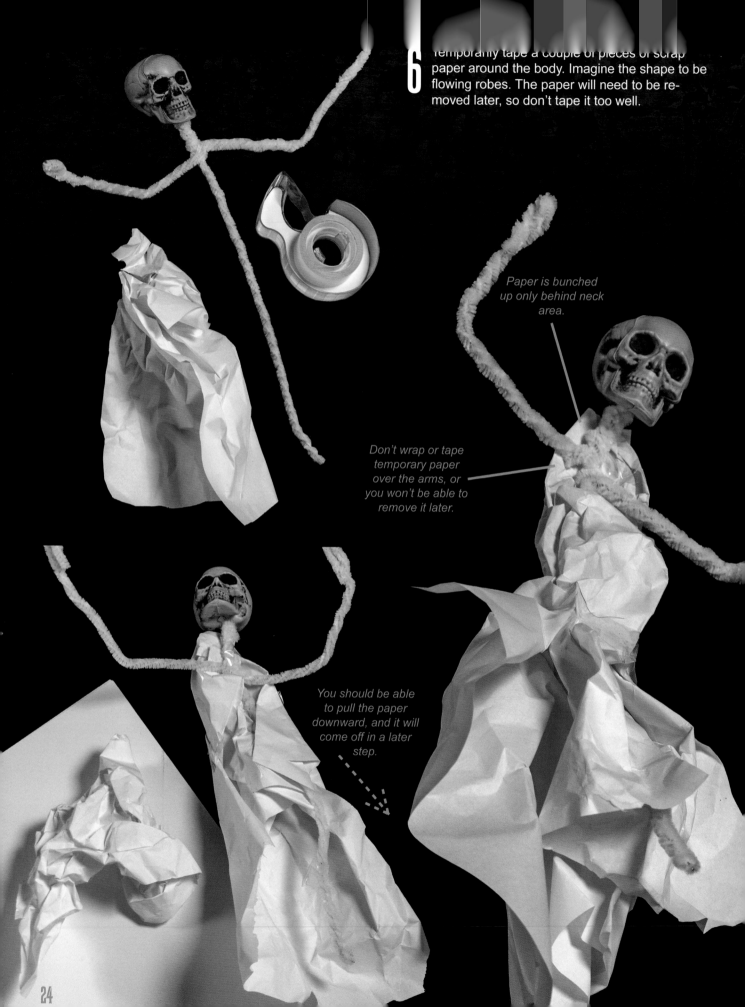

6 Temporarily tape a couple of pieces of scrap paper around the body. Imagine the shape to be flowing robes. The paper will need to be removed later, so don't tape it too well.

Paper is bunched up only behind neck area.

Don't wrap or tape temporary paper over the arms, or you won't be able to remove it later.

You should be able to pull the paper downward, and it will come off in a later step.

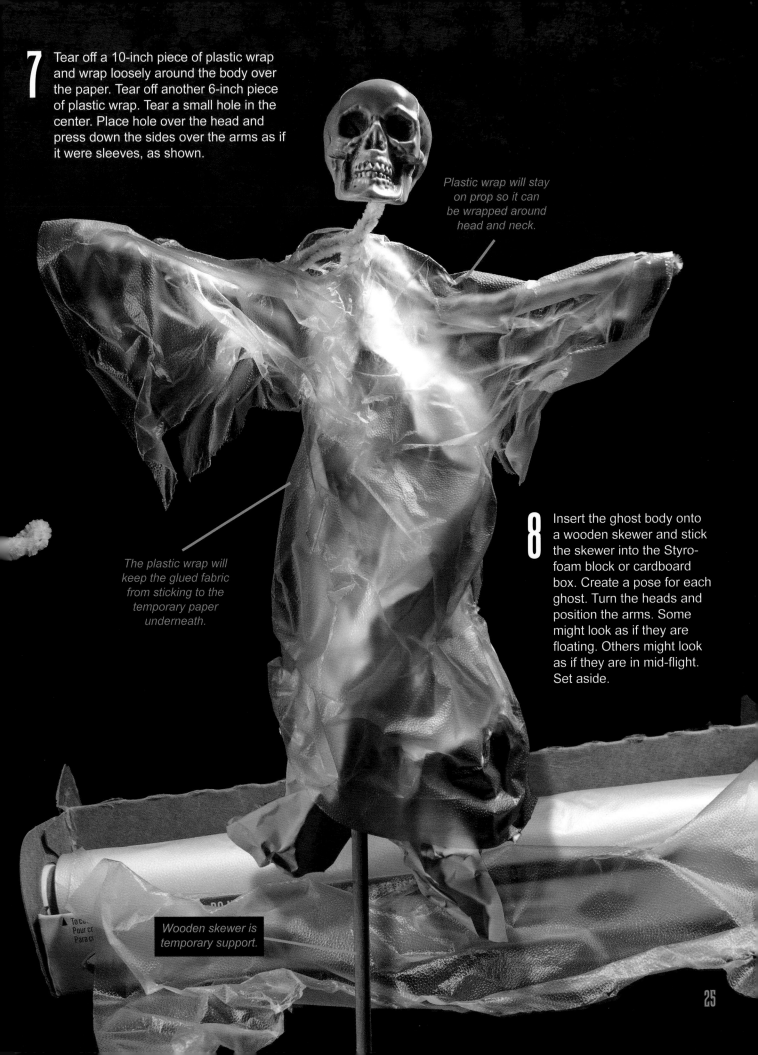

7 Tear off a 10-inch piece of plastic wrap and wrap loosely around the body over the paper. Tear off another 6-inch piece of plastic wrap. Tear a small hole in the center. Place hole over the head and press down the sides over the arms as if it were sleeves, as shown.

Plastic wrap will stay on prop so it can be wrapped around head and neck.

The plastic wrap will keep the glued fabric from sticking to the temporary paper underneath.

8 Insert the ghost body onto a wooden skewer and stick the skewer into the Styrofoam block or cardboard box. Create a pose for each ghost. Turn the heads and position the arms. Some might look as if they are floating. Others might look as if they are in mid-flight. Set aside.

Wooden skewer is temporary support.

9 Cut several pieces of cheesecloth approximately 5–8 inches long and 3–5 inches wide. Pull on each piece of cheesecloth to distress the threads a little. Add approximately 2 ounces of water to bowl. Mix in approximately 2 ounces of school glue and stir.

10 Take a plastic garbage bag and crumple it up on top of the table. The plastic bag needs to have an uneven surface of small hills and valleys. This will be the work surface to lay the glued cheesecloth pieces on. The pieces should dry in wavy shapes.

11 Dip into the glue liquid one piece of cut cheesecloth at a time. Stretch out the fabric and lay over the plastic trash bag so parts are both up and down on the folds. Once dry, these pieces can be removed from the plastic, and they will retain their flowing shapes. Let the cheesecloth dry overnight. Make at least three or four per ghost.

Shape the cheesecloth to look windblown and wavy. Once the pieces are dry, they will be attached to miniature ghost body to give it a floating or flying look.

ELMER'S®

WASHABLE, NO RUN

SCHOOL GLUE

#1 Teacher Brand®

Safe | Nontoxic
32 fl oz (946 mL)

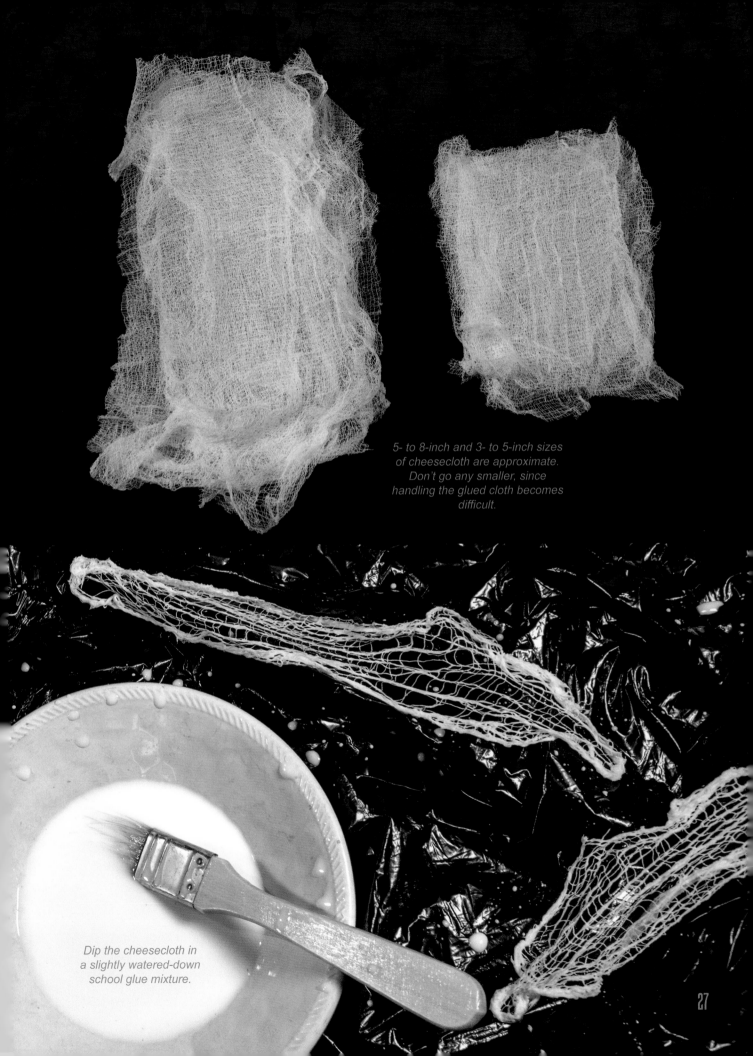

5- to 8-inch and 3- to 5-inch sizes of cheesecloth are approximate. Don't go any smaller, since handling the glued cloth becomes difficult.

Dip the cheesecloth in a slightly watered-down school glue mixture.

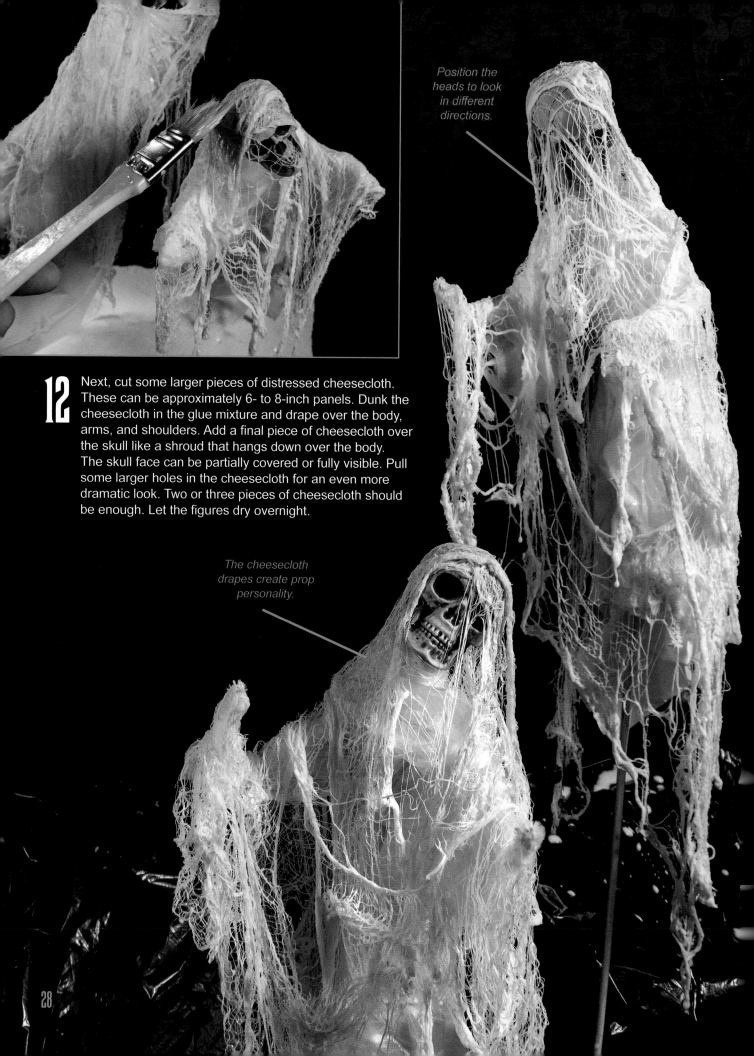

Position the heads to look in different directions.

12 Next, cut some larger pieces of distressed cheesecloth. These can be approximately 6- to 8-inch panels. Dunk the cheesecloth in the glue mixture and drape over the body, arms, and shoulders. Add a final piece of cheesecloth over the skull like a shroud that hangs down over the body. The skull face can be partially covered or fully visible. Pull some larger holes in the cheesecloth for an even more dramatic look. Two or three pieces of cheesecloth should be enough. Let the figures dry overnight.

The cheesecloth drapes create prop personality.

Let these dry completely overnight, before removing from skewers.

Distressed strands of cheesecloth look amazing stretched over the skull.

Make a really big hole in the middle of the cheesecloth and drape over arms, with strands hanging down.

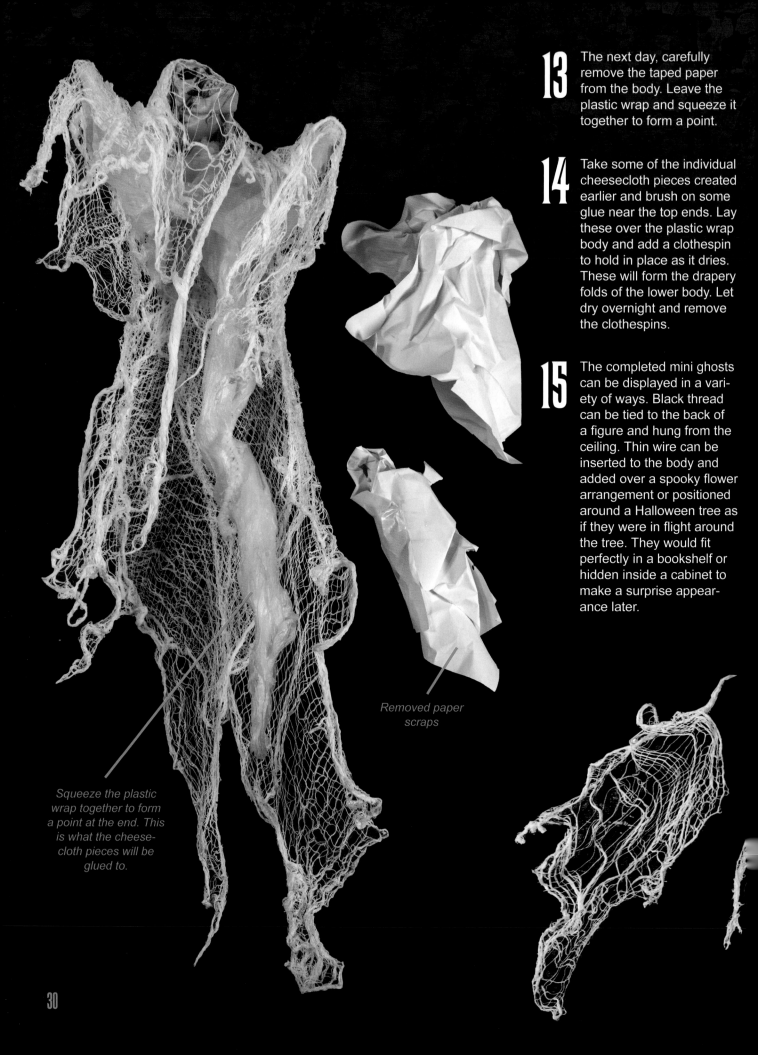

13 The next day, carefully remove the taped paper from the body. Leave the plastic wrap and squeeze it together to form a point.

14 Take some of the individual cheesecloth pieces created earlier and brush on some glue near the top ends. Lay these over the plastic wrap body and add a clothespin to hold in place as it dries. These will form the drapery folds of the lower body. Let dry overnight and remove the clothespins.

15 The completed mini ghosts can be displayed in a variety of ways. Black thread can be tied to the back of a figure and hung from the ceiling. Thin wire can be inserted to the body and added over a spooky flower arrangement or positioned around a Halloween tree as if they were in flight around the tree. They would fit perfectly in a bookshelf or hidden inside a cabinet to make a surprise appearance later.

Removed paper scraps

Squeeze the plastic wrap together to form a point at the end. This is what the cheese-cloth pieces will be glued to.

TIP: These would not work well outdoors.
Moisture would remove the stiffness of
the fabric and cause it to sag.

*Hold onto the dried
cheesecloth section
as the clothespin is
removed, so the section
doesn't peel off.*

Booooo!

Make a Flower BOOquet

The small size of these ghosts makes them excellent additions to flower arrangements. Whether one ghost or three, add a little spirit to your Halloween wreaths, trees, flowers, or any other decor that needs a lift!

Wooden Pumpkin Display

YOU WILL NEED: several sizes pre-cut wooden tree slices, a ruler, pumpkin prints printed on copy paper to match the size of the tree slices, Matte Mod Podge, a brush, paper towel, a bowl of water and rag, wood glue, tooth-picks, $^{11}\!/_{64}$-inch drill bit *(or one slightly larger than a toothpick),* drill, some approximately ½-inch sticks from the yard, sanding block, hanging brackets *(optional)*

These wooden pumpkins fit right in to a primitive or farmhouse décor. Their flat proportions mean they can be hung on a wall, used as a table centerpiece, or set out on a mantle.

1 Tree slices come in a variety of sizes. Shown here are the 4.5-, 6.5-, 3.75-, and 3.5-inch sizes. These can be found at hobby stores or online from a variety of craft retailers and are sold as a group by size.

3.5 inch

3.75 inch

inch

These Fuyit wood slices were purchased online. Search for "Unfinished natural tree slice" under Crafts. They come in packs listed by size.

2 Measure the tree slice width. Print the template with the closest size, slightly bigger than wood. If using this as a table-top display where both sides are visible, you will need a print for both sides.

3 Cut out the borders of each print. The print should be larger than the wood.

4 Use a brush to add Mod Podge up to the bark edge of one side of a tree slice. With print side down, press the print firmly onto the wood surface. Try not to let it slide around as you gently push out any air bubbles. A stiff card or an old credit card is great for pressing the print onto the wood surface. Use a paper towel to wipe any excess glue off the wood bark on the opposite side.

5 Set the wet glued wood pieces aside and allow them to dry overnight.

6 Once dry, either do step 4 for the opposite side of wood *(for two-sided display piece)*, or, for a wall hanging pumpkin display, continue to next step.

Use Matte Mod Podge for less shine on the rustic wood pieces.

If the bark is shedding too much, you can Mod Podge over it. Otherwise, avoid getting glue on the bark edges. The bark will look more natural if left as is.

PLAID
CS11302

MOD PODGE®
MATTE-MAT-MATE

Water-based glue, sealer & finish
Colle, scellant et fini à base d'eau
Pega

Use a stiff board or old credit card to help press out any bubbles from the print.

Clean up any glue drips with a paper towel.

7 Place a wet rag over each print to soak for a couple of minutes.

8 Remove rag and pull off any paper corners not glued down. Using your fingertips, gently begin rolling off the paper from the wood. The print ink should stay on the wood while the paper comes off. Don't rub too vigorously or the ink will come off also. Keep in mind that these are a rustic design, so they don't have to be perfect. Once all the paper has been removed, while still wet, add another thin coat of Mod Podge over the print and let dry.

The best way to remove the paper from the print is using your fingers. Keep the fingertips flat against the wood and roll the paper off. Don't dig into the print or the ink will come off also.

Make sure the whole print is completely wet before trying to remove the paper.

Gently wipe off any remaining paper pieces from the surface.

A dry pumpkin print will show some wood through and have a rustic appearance.

39

9 Find some sticks about ½ inch thick from the yard. Cut or break them to any length you want for each pumpkin. It can be long or short. Use a sanding block to smooth out the end of the stick that will attach to each pumpkin edge.

Drill small hole in center edge of wood.

Use a strong wood glue to hold the wooden parts together.

Drill small hole in center of stick end that will attach to wood.

10 Use a small drill bit *(¹¹⁄₆₄-inch size)* that will allow a toothpick to fit into both the top pumpkin edge and the stick center for added support. Make the drill hole approximately ¾ inch deep. If the pumpkin wood starts to split, stop drilling. You can shorten the toothpick, so it fits in both the stick and the pumpkin edge. Add wood glue to each end of the toothpick. Gently push one end of the toothpick into the stick and the other end into the pumpkin edge. Let glue dry completely. Add a small amount of wood glue over the wood split, if needed.

If the wood starts to split, fill in the crack with some wood glue and shorten the toothpick to fit the hole depth.

¹¹⁄₆₄-inch drill bit

Any kind of toothpick can be used. Shorten length, as needed, to fit in holes. Both wood parts should fit snuggly together.

Add generous amount of glue to the toothpick before inserting in into the wood.

11 If the pumpkins are to be hung, add a picture hook to the back of each pumpkin and glue in place.

12 If the pumpkins are to be displayed standing up, use some strong wood glue to attach to a wooden base. We used a larger branch as a base and attached the pumpkins to the top edge along the length. Attach a smaller branch for support, if needed.

Optionally, a second branch was hot-glued to the main stick for balance.

Find an interesting branch for the pumpkins to sit on.

This display would look good on a mantle or as a table centerpiece!

Hot glue may be used to temporarily attach the pumpkins to the stick.

Add glue where pumpkin touches the branch.

41

Pumpkin Face #1 Template: This template is meant to look imperfect and rustic. Scale the image, larger or smaller, so that it fits slightly larger than the wood slice it will go on. Print on standard copy paper.

Pumpkin Face #2 Template: This template is meant to look imperfect and rustic. Scale the image, larger or smaller, so that it fits slightly larger than the wood slice it will go on. Print on standard copy paper.

Pumpkin Face #3 Template: This template is meant to look imperfect and rustic. Scale the image, larger or smaller, so that it fits slightly larger than the wood slice it will go on. Print on standard copy paper.

Jack-o'-lanterns grin throughout the season!

Crazy for Crepe!

Multi-Use Crepe Paper Strands

YOU WILL NEED: crepe paper rolls in your choice of black, orange, gray, or greens; small sponge or folded-up paper towel *(slightly moistened);* black yarn; and scissors

Once you learn the basics of how this material is used, you could do it while watching your favorite seasonal movies. You will want to make a lot, since this very versatile material can be used in a multitude of ways. Best of all, crepe paper is very inexpensive and comes in many different colors. It can be found at Dollar Stores or ordered online. Crepe paper usually comes two rolls per bag. Look for them in party supply areas.

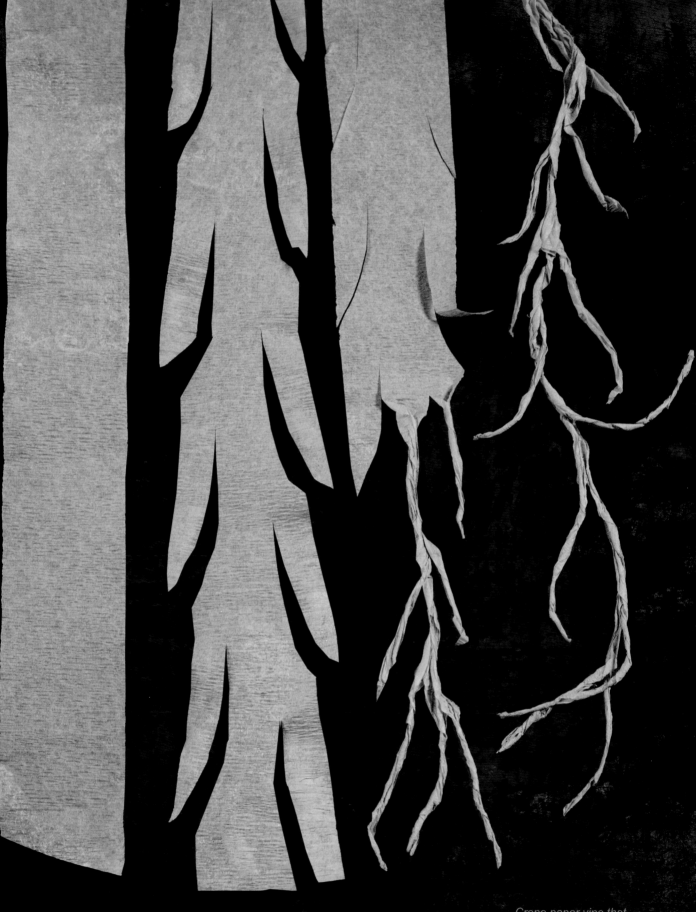

Crepe paper strip

Alternating cuts on crepe paper

Finger-twisted crepe paper

Crepe paper vine that can be used in a variety of ways

Crepe Paper Method 1: Rolled Strands

Method 1: Rolled Strands

Use *method 1* when you want a distinctive, creepy vine or witchy hair appearance to the crepe paper.

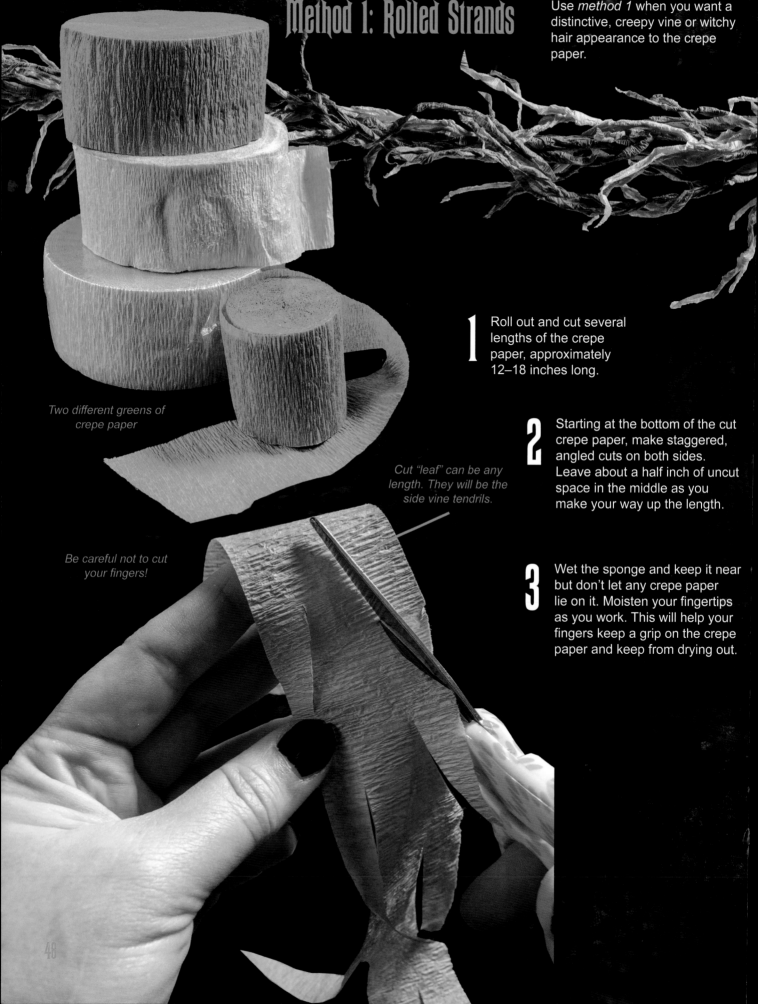

Two different greens of crepe paper

Cut "leaf" can be any length. They will be the side vine tendrils.

Be careful not to cut your fingers!

1 Roll out and cut several lengths of the crepe paper, approximately 12–18 inches long.

2 Starting at the bottom of the cut crepe paper, make staggered, angled cuts on both sides. Leave about a half inch of uncut space in the middle as you make your way up the length.

3 Wet the sponge and keep it near but don't let any crepe paper lie on it. Moisten your fingertips as you work. This will help your fingers keep a grip on the crepe paper and keep from drying out.

4 Again, starting at the bottom of the crepe paper, take one of the cut leaves and roll it between your fingers to form a rough vine. Continue to do each leaf the same way, working your way up. Also, roll the center stem section as you go upward the same way as the leaves. Keep moistening your fingertips; it will help with the twisting.

5 Make as many vine sections as you want. In this instance, we created two green variations for a creepy swamp theme.

Moist sponge helps the fingertips work the crepe paper.

Green Crepe Paper:

Crepe paper in multi-color greens would be great for seaweed, jungle vines, or even a harvest theme.

Crepe Paper Method 2: Pinch Strands

Use *method 2* when you must make a LOT of crepe paper vines. In a mass of crepe paper, no one will see individual strands. They will see a wall of colorful paper décor. This method creates the individual pieces quicker. Two different strands can also be gently twisted together to make dual color vines that work well in a theme.

1 Roll out and cut several lengths of the crepe paper, approximately 12–18 inches long.

2 Starting at the bottom of the crepe paper, make staggered, angled cuts on both sides, the same as in *method 1*.

3 Take each leaf and quickly pinch *(wrinkle)* the paper. Work your way up from the leaf end to branch, and on to the next leaf up the chain. The vine will need to be untwisted every now and then, since turning it from side to side will curl up the unworked end of the vine. After a little practice, you won't even have to keep your eyes on the piece as you work.

The pinch strands method looks great when multiple vines are displayed together. The pinched paper will bulk up and stand apart just enough to create the vine effect.

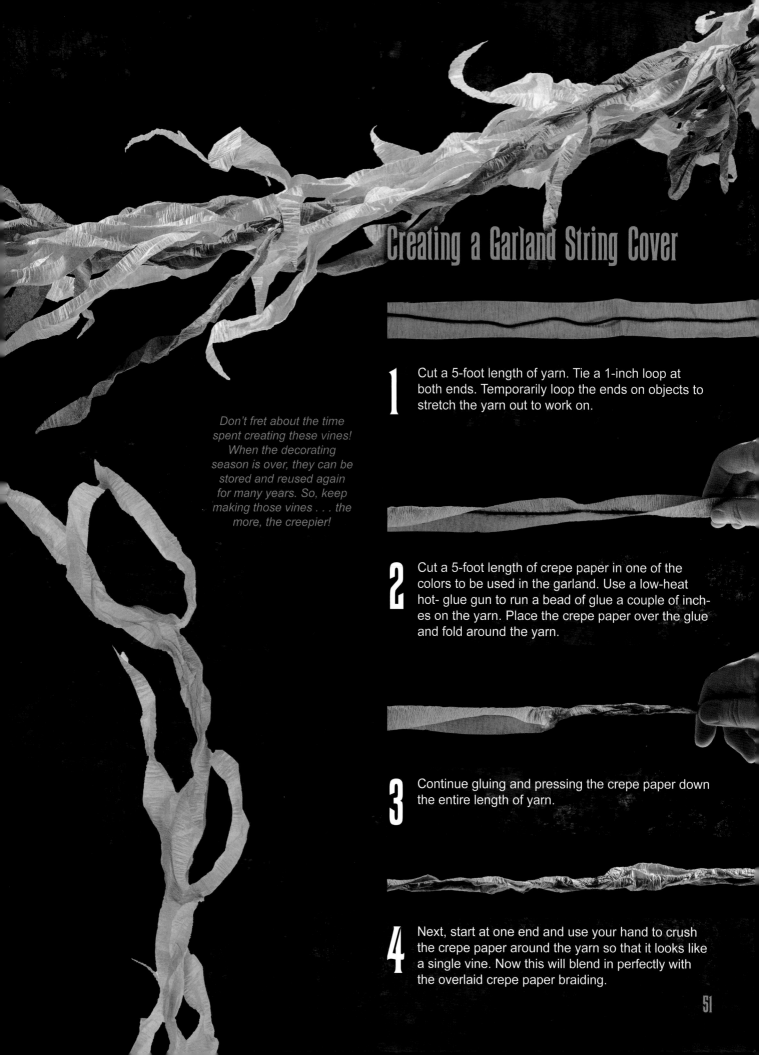

Creating a Garland String Cover

Don't fret about the time spent creating these vines! When the decorating season is over, they can be stored and reused again for many years. So, keep making those vines . . . the more, the creepier!

1 Cut a 5-foot length of yarn. Tie a 1-inch loop at both ends. Temporarily loop the ends on objects to stretch the yarn out to work on.

2 Cut a 5-foot length of crepe paper in one of the colors to be used in the garland. Use a low-heat hot- glue gun to run a bead of glue a couple of inches on the yarn. Place the crepe paper over the glue and fold around the yarn.

3 Continue gluing and pressing the crepe paper down the entire length of yarn.

4 Next, start at one end and use your hand to crush the crepe paper around the yarn so that it looks like a single vine. Now this will blend in perfectly with the overlaid crepe paper braiding.

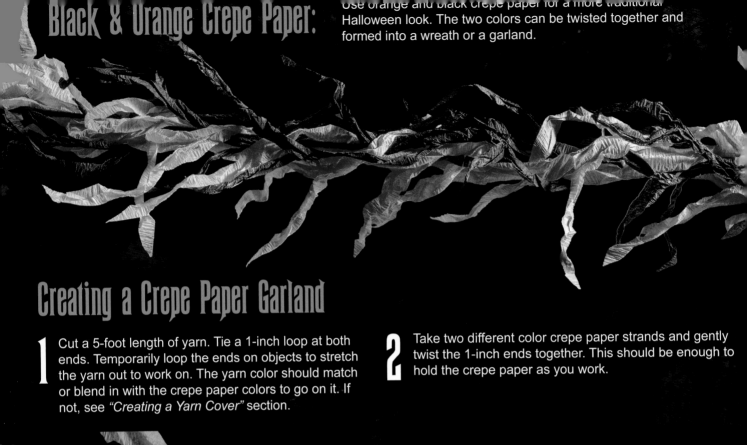

Black & Orange Crepe Paper:

Use orange and black crepe paper for a more traditional Halloween look. The two colors can be twisted together and formed into a wreath or a garland.

Creating a Crepe Paper Garland

1 Cut a 5-foot length of yarn. Tie a 1-inch loop at both ends. Temporarily loop the ends on objects to stretch the yarn out to work on. The yarn color should match or blend in with the crepe paper colors to go on it. If not, see *"Creating a Yarn Cover"* section.

2 Take two different color crepe paper strands and gently twist the 1-inch ends together. This should be enough to hold the crepe paper as you work.

Twisted ends

Loose braiding around yarn

WARNING! If you have cats, you might want to keep the crepe paper up high. Cats love the sound and feel of crepe paper and will chew it up or eat it!

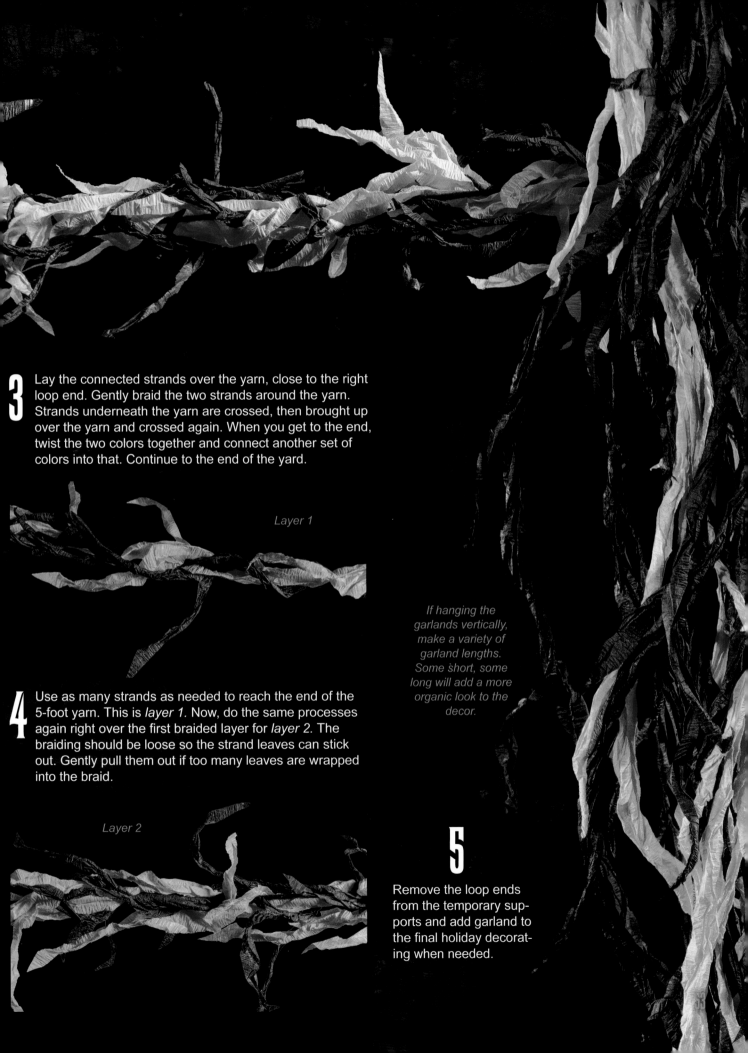

3 Lay the connected strands over the yarn, close to the right loop end. Gently braid the two strands around the yarn. Strands underneath the yarn are crossed, then brought up over the yarn and crossed again. When you get to the end, twist the two colors together and connect another set of colors into that. Continue to the end of the yard.

Layer 1

4 Use as many strands as needed to reach the end of the 5-foot yarn. This is *layer 1*. Now, do the same processes again right over the first braided layer for *layer 2*. The braiding should be loose so the strand leaves can stick out. Gently pull them out if too many leaves are wrapped into the braid.

If hanging the garlands vertically, make a variety of garland lengths. Some short, some long will add a more organic look to the decor.

Layer 2

5 Remove the loop ends from the temporary supports and add garland to the final holiday decorating when needed.

Black Crepe Paper:

Use a group of all black (*or black and purple*) crepe paper strands for a dark and moody, gothic look. Hang several strands from a chandelier or lay them along a table as a runner, with other props placed in and around it. These could also be used as curtains or hung from a doorway to make a decorative entrance.

Gray Crepe Paper:

Using all gray crepe paper would create a true
Spanish moss appearance or add to a ghostly,
decrepit feel to a room. Pair the stands with dried
flowers in a vase for the family crypt decor.

The twisted strands can also be used to make a wreath. Start with a store-bought wire wreath frame as a base. Gently twist the vines around the frame until it is the size needed.

TIP: This twisted material could also be used to top Halloween gift boxes or as "hair" on a handcrafted doll prop.

TIP: Storing the crepe paper works best when put inside a plastic container with a lid. Don't press them down. Gently lay them in the container until it is full. Without the container, extreme heat, or damp, can cause the crepe paper to wilt. If this happens, just re-fluff the strands when you put them up again. Using a storage container is the best method of protecting the crepe paper.

Crepe paper brings out the crazy in everyone!

58

Paper Candlesticks

YOU WILL NEED: candle templates printed on a heavier weight paper like index paper in 8.5 x 11 size, X-acto knife or scissors, Tacky Glue, ruler, cutting board, 1-inch-diameter PVC pipe or other similar size dowel rod for rolling the paper, Scotch tape, toothpick, and a coffee stirrer or kid's juice straw

Paper candlesticks are a safe substitute for real candles, with a nod to the old-fashioned Halloween decorating of the 1920s and '30s. One fun surprise about this project is that all the white areas of the paper will glow brilliantly under black light!

"Builder, baker and the candlestick maker..."

A Halloween crafter wears many hats!

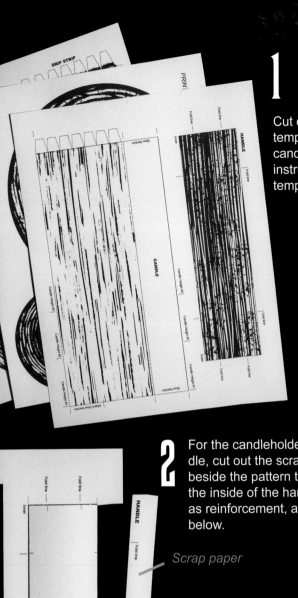

1

Cut out candle templates for each candle, following instructions on the template.

Digital template files can also be downloaded from our website.

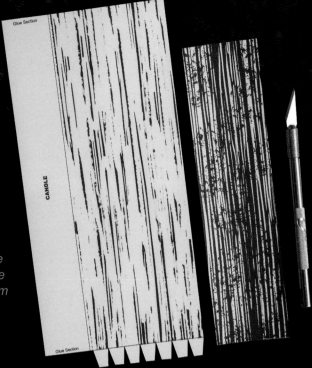

2

For the candleholder's handle, cut out the scrap piece beside the pattern to glue to the inside of the handle piece as reinforcement, as shown below.

Scrap paper

Handle part

3

Fold the two long sides of the handle and use Tacky Glue on both sides. Sandwich the glued scrap paper inside and press closed. Then, fold the two ends of the handle as shown. Set aside.

Folded handle part

Scrap paper

Unfolded handle part

Glued scrap paper

Glued handle part

Final handle

Tacky Glue is perfect for working with paper. It dries fast, yet still flexible.

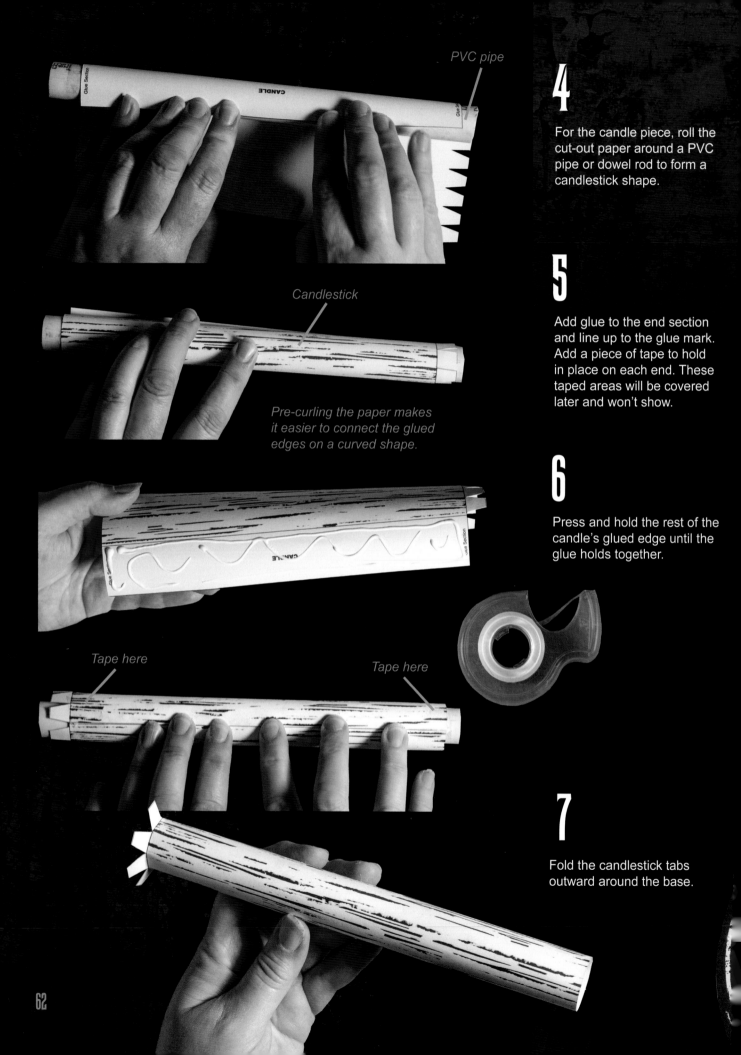

PVC pipe

4

For the candle piece, roll the cut-out paper around a PVC pipe or dowel rod to form a candlestick shape.

5

Add glue to the end section and line up to the glue mark. Add a piece of tape to hold in place on each end. These taped areas will be covered later and won't show.

Candlestick

Pre-curling the paper makes it easier to connect the glued edges on a curved shape.

6

Press and hold the rest of the candle's glued edge until the glue holds together.

Tape here

Tape here

7

Fold the candlestick tabs outward around the base.

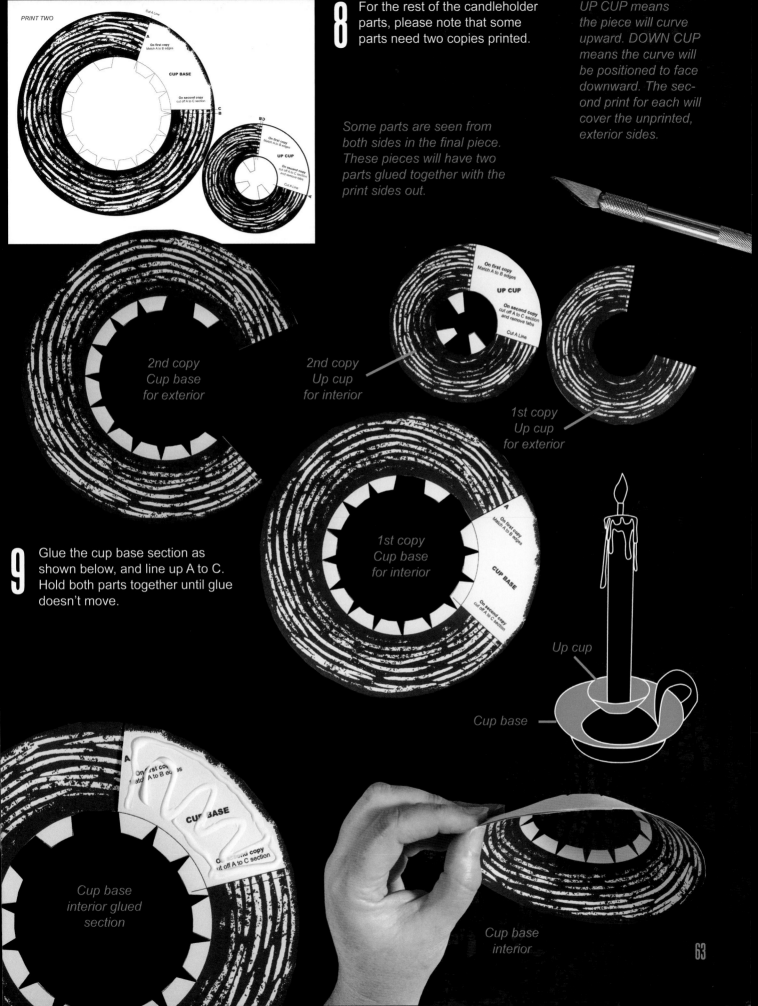

PRINT TWO

8 For the rest of the candleholder parts, please note that some parts need two copies printed.

UP CUP means the piece will curve upward. DOWN CUP means the curve will be positioned to face downward. The second print for each will cover the unprinted, exterior sides.

Some parts are seen from both sides in the final piece. These pieces will have two parts glued together with the print sides out.

2nd copy Cup base for exterior

2nd copy Up cup for interior

1st copy Up cup for exterior

9 Glue the cup base section as shown below, and line up A to C. Hold both parts together until glue doesn't move.

1st copy Cup base for interior

Up cup

Cup base

Cup base interior glued section

Cup base interior

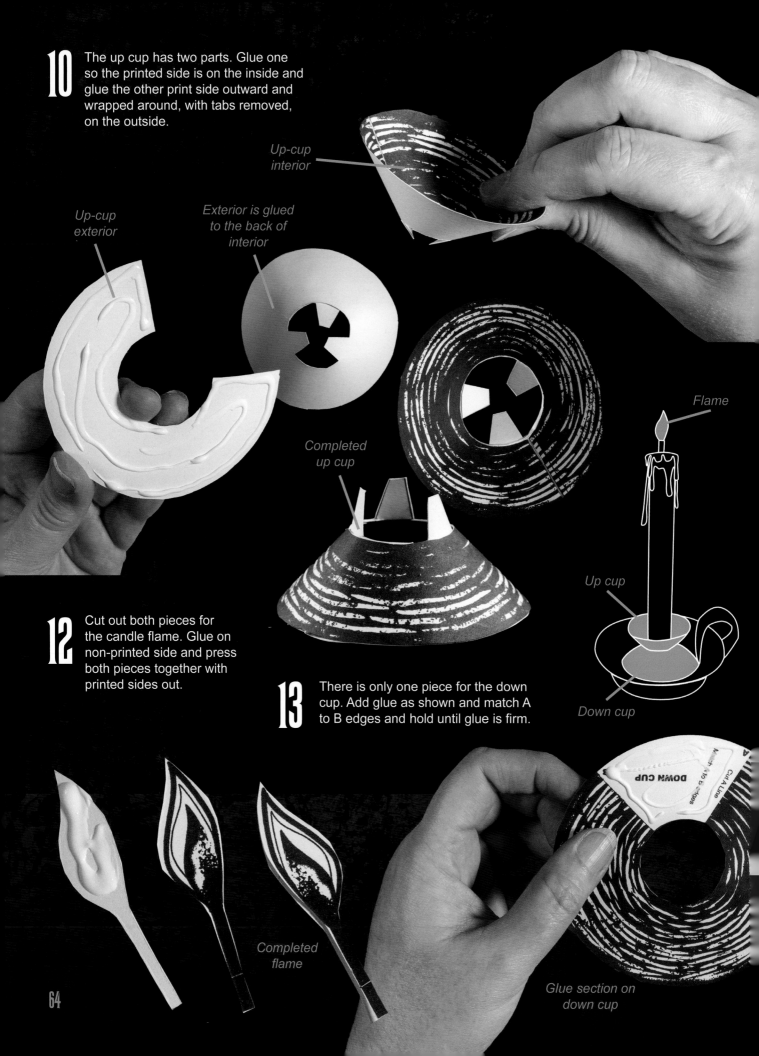

10 The up cup has two parts. Glue one so the printed side is on the inside and glue the other print side outward and wrapped around, with tabs removed, on the outside.

Up-cup interior

Up-cup exterior

Exterior is glued to the back of interior

Completed up cup

Flame

Up cup

Down cup

12 Cut out both pieces for the candle flame. Glue on non-printed side and press both pieces together with printed sides out.

13 There is only one piece for the down cup. Add glue as shown and match A to B edges and hold until glue is firm.

Completed flame

DOWN CUP

Glue section on down cup

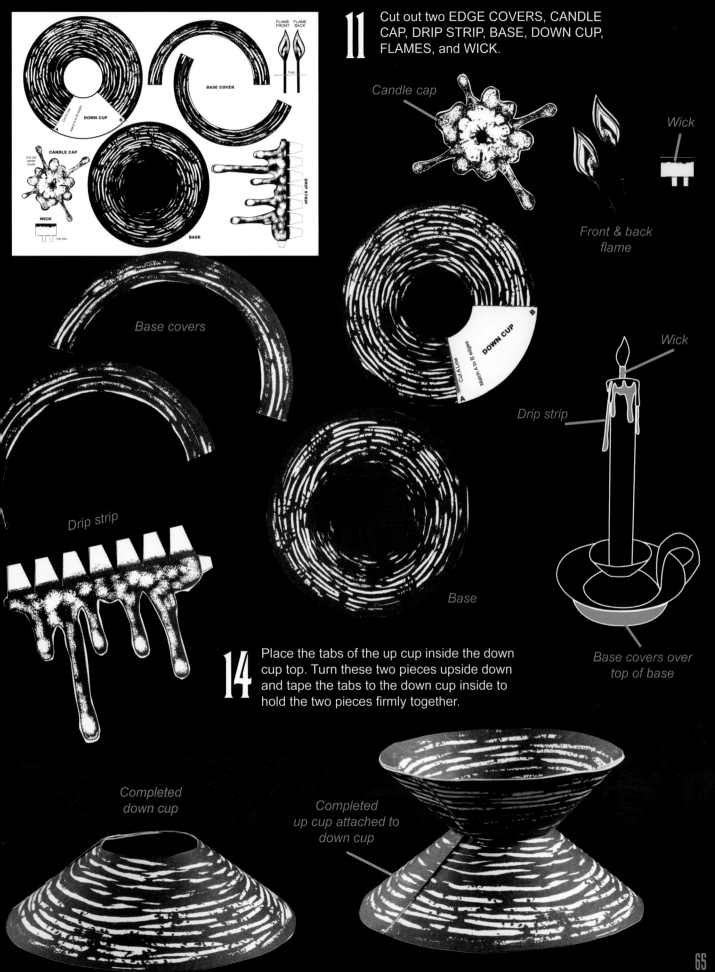

11 Cut out two EDGE COVERS, CANDLE CAP, DRIP STRIP, BASE, DOWN CUP, FLAMES, and WICK.

Candle cap

Wick

Front & back flame

Base covers

Wick

Drip strip

Drip strip

Base

Base covers over top of base

14 Place the tabs of the up cup inside the down cup top. Turn these two pieces upside down and tape the tabs to the down cup inside to hold the two pieces firmly together.

Completed down cup

Completed up cup attached to down cup

15 Wrap the wick around the coffee stirrer or small straw to curve the paper. Glue or tape the wick edge to hold shape. Bend the tabs outward. Set aside.

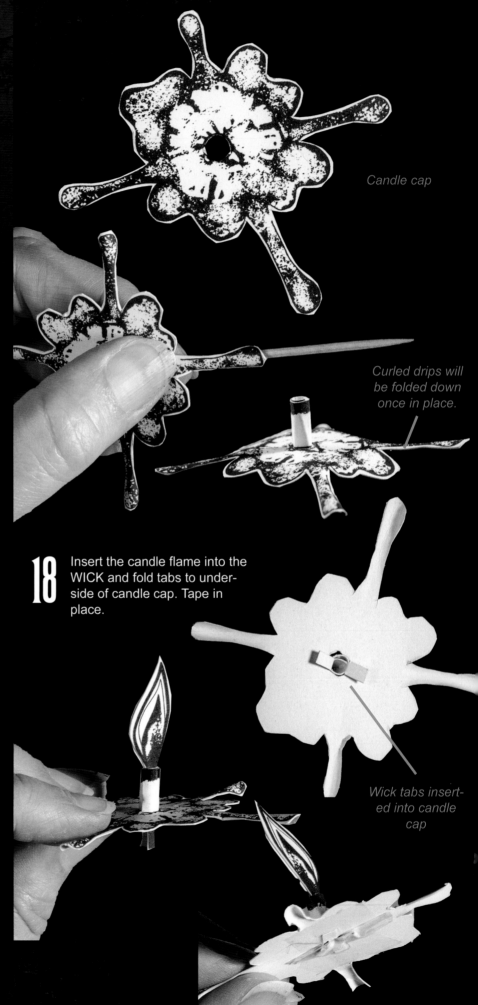

Candle cap

Curled drips will be folded down once in place.

16 Use a toothpick to curve each of the candle drips extensions.

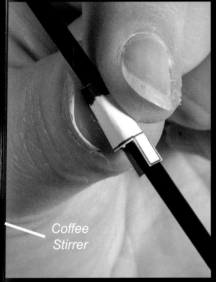

Coffee Stirrer

18 Insert the candle flame into the WICK and fold tabs to underside of candle cap. Tape in place.

Wick tabs inserted into candle cap

17 Insert the wick tabs into the candle cap hole. Tape in place.

Wick tabs

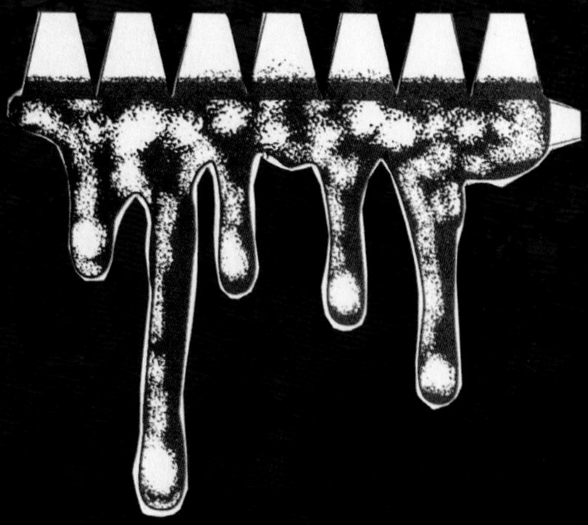

19 Use a ruler edge to fold the candle drip tab row.

20 Roll the tab row into a circle and tape the top.

21 Use a toothpick to shape a curve for each of the drip extensions as shown.

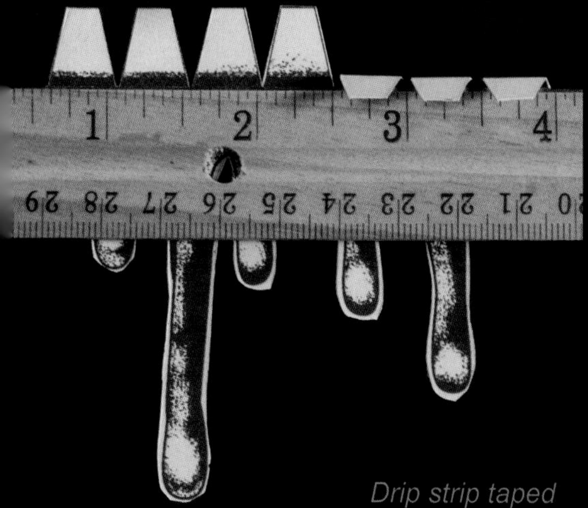

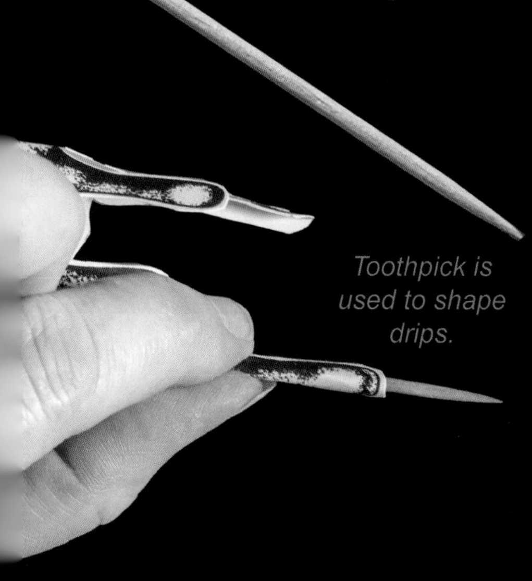

22 Tape the candlestick tabs to the non-printed side of the cup base.

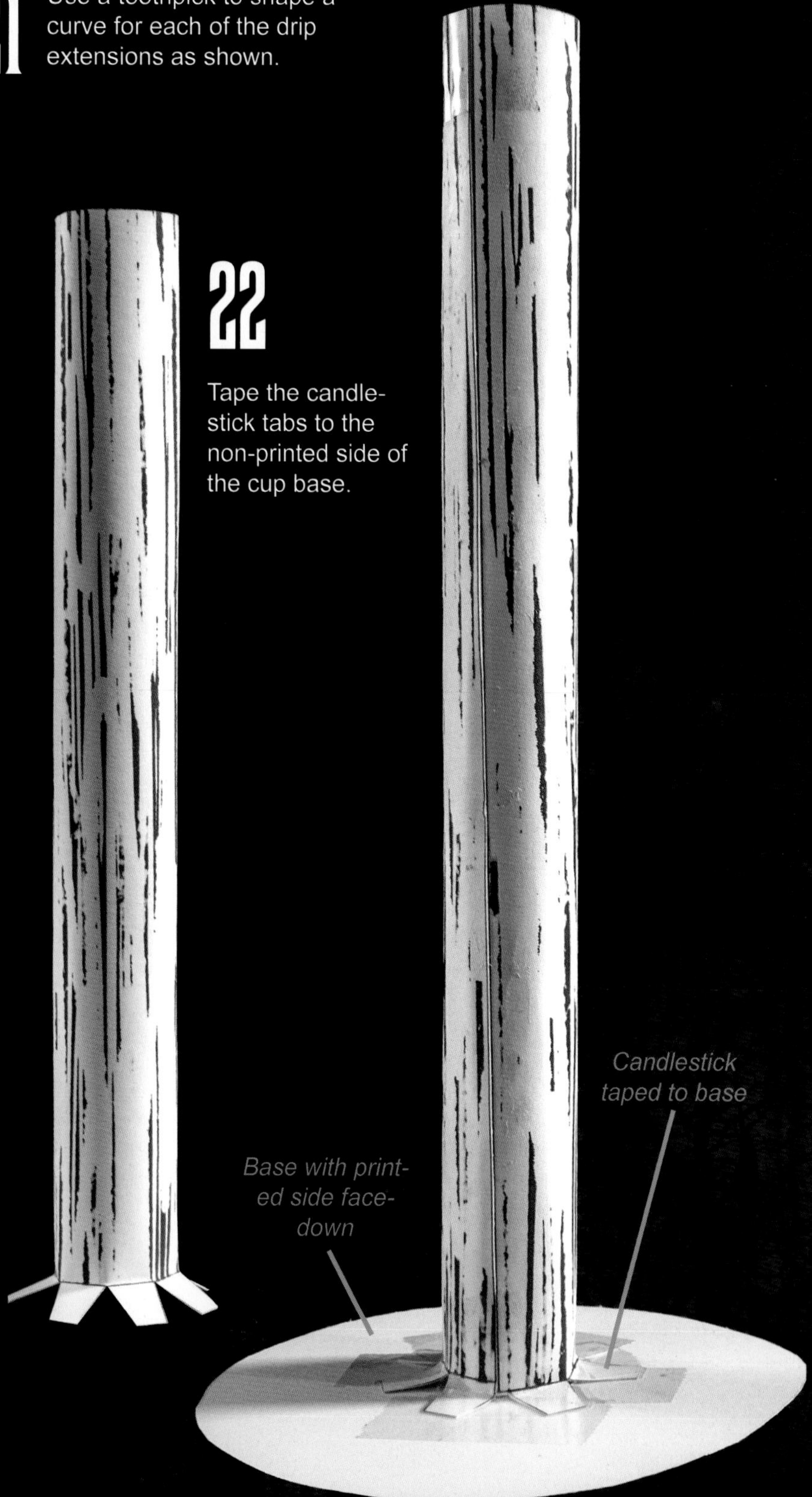

Drip strip taped together

Toothpick is used to shape drips.

Candlestick taped to base

Base with printed side face-down

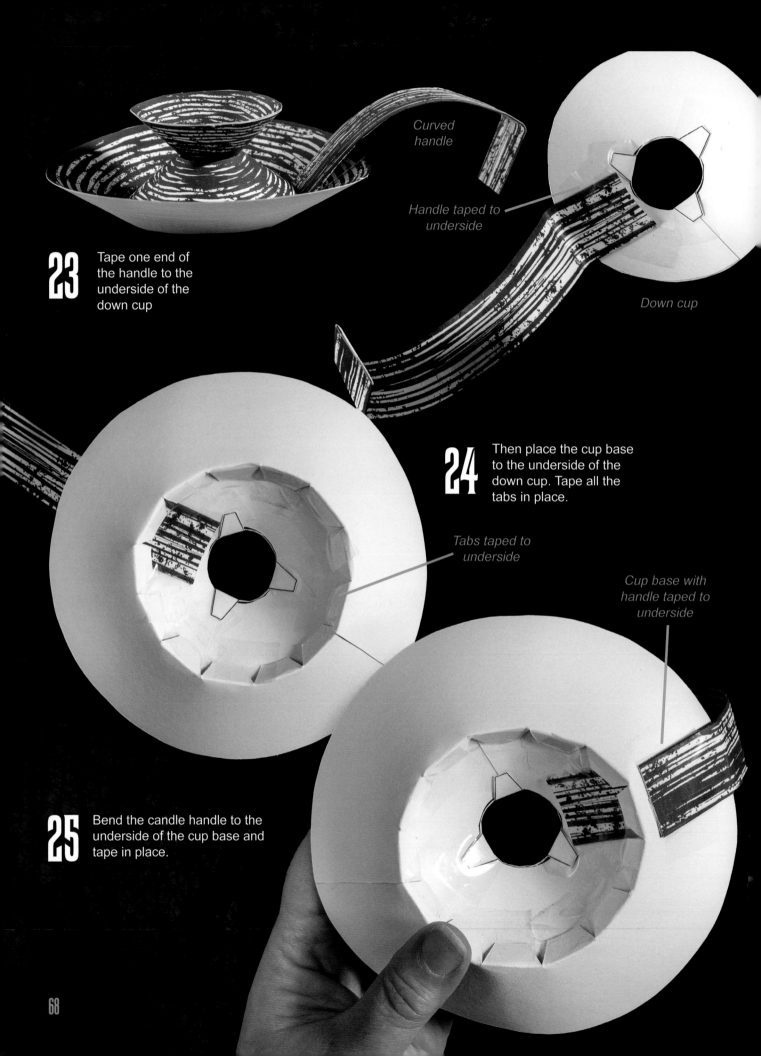

Curved handle

Handle taped to underside

23 Tape one end of the handle to the underside of the down cup

Down cup

24 Then place the cup base to the underside of the down cup. Tape all the tabs in place.

Tabs taped to underside

Cup base with handle taped to underside

25 Bend the candle handle to the underside of the cup base and tape in place.

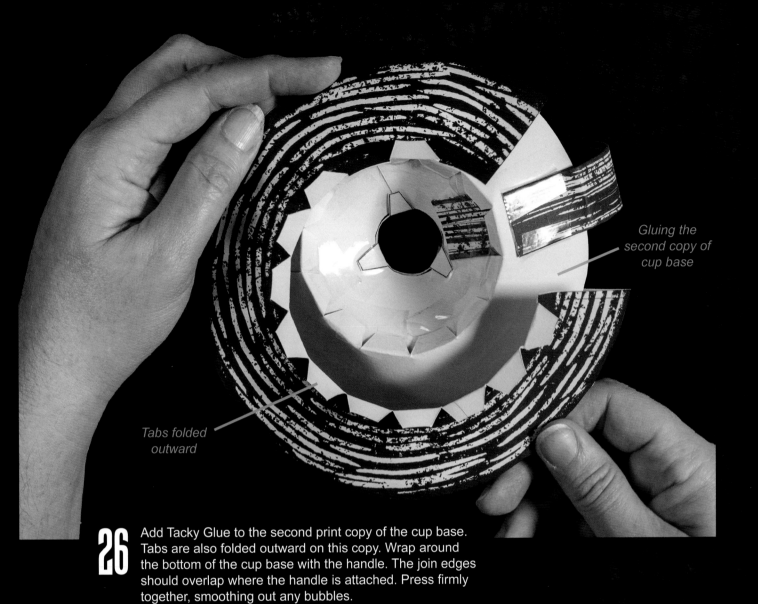

Gluing the second copy of cup base

Tabs folded outward

26 Add Tacky Glue to the second print copy of the cup base. Tabs are also folded outward on this copy. Wrap around the bottom of the cup base with the handle. The join edges should overlap where the handle is attached. Press firmly together, smoothing out any bubbles.

Join cut edges at the back of the handle.

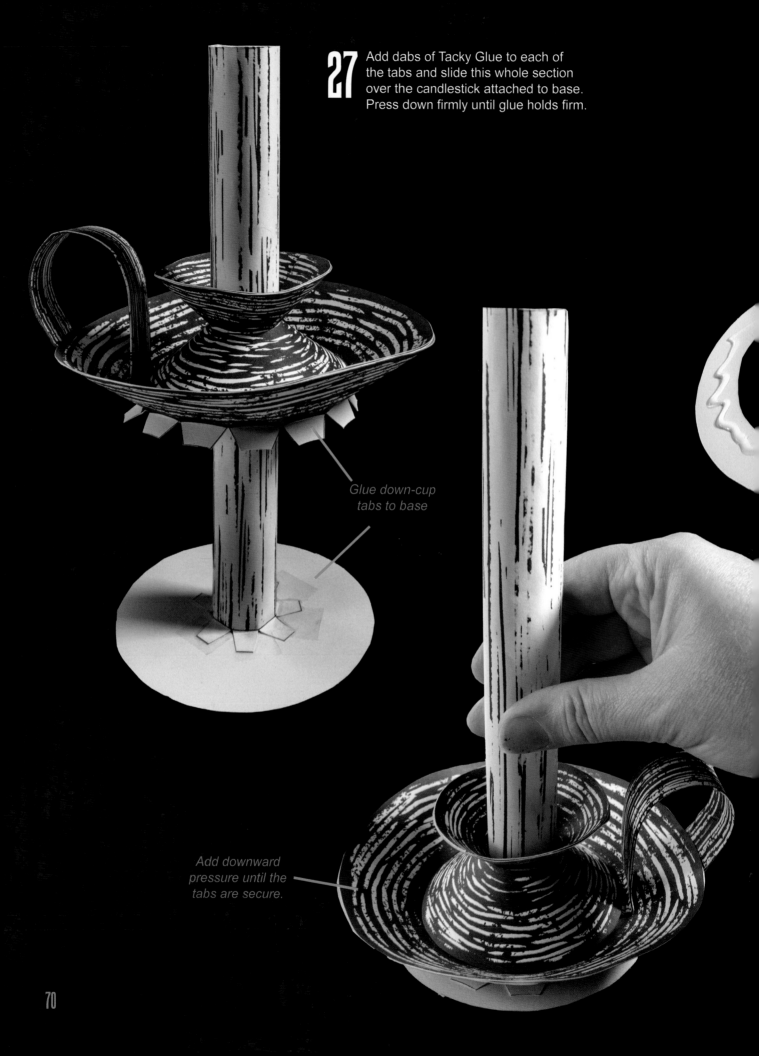

27 Add dabs of Tacky Glue to each of the tabs and slide this whole section over the candlestick attached to base. Press down firmly until glue holds firm.

Glue down-cup tabs to base

Add downward pressure until the tabs are secure.

Candle cap edges are bent over candle top

Base covers hide the tabs and finish the look of the base.

28 Add glue to both non-printed sides of the edge covers. Place these over the base with print-sides up. Press down around edge until glue is firm.

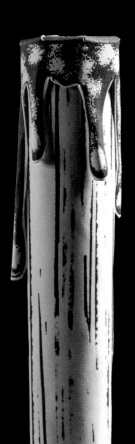

29 Add small amount of Tacky Glue to bottom of candle drips piece and add to top of CANDLESTICK. The candle drip extension will sit above surface of candlestick as shown.

30 Add small amount of glue to underside of candle cap and place over candle drips piece. Fold down rounded edges as shown at top right.

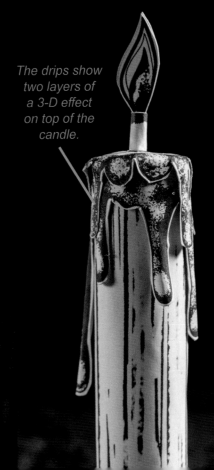

The drips show two layers of a 3-D effect on top of the candle.

The candlestick height can be cut to different sizes for added interest.

31 To make simple candlestick holder, use only the up- and down-cups section glued over print-side up base piece.

Simple candlestick holder

Base is print side up on the simple candlestick.

Complete paper candle with holder

73

Simple Candlestick

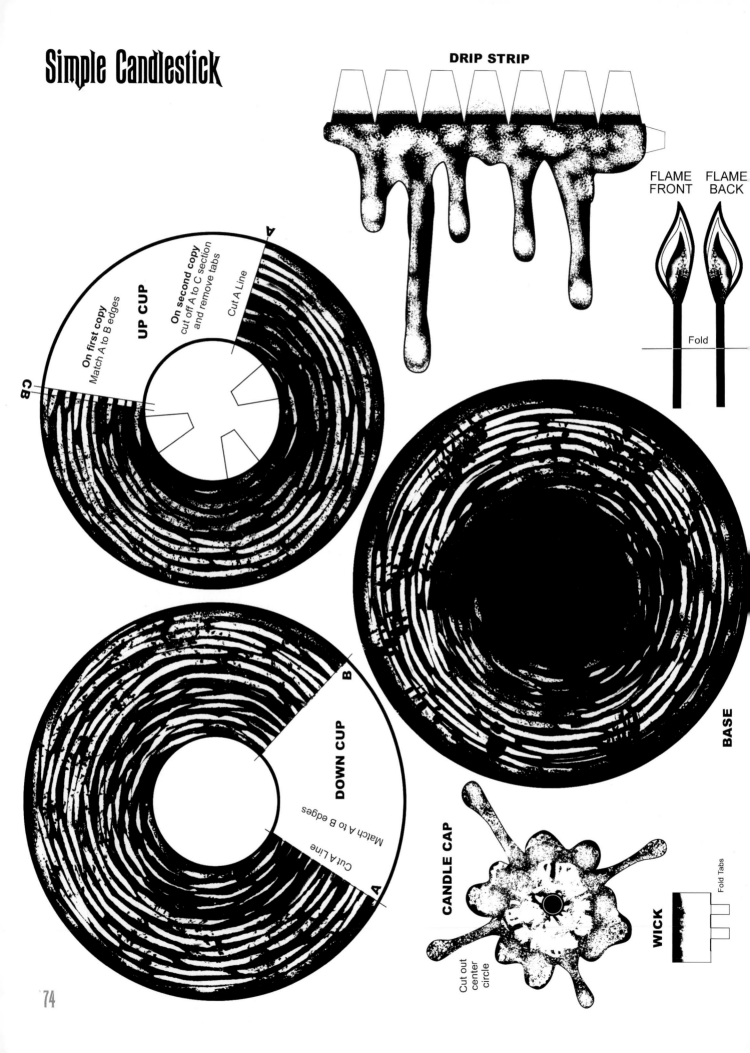

DRIP STRIP

FLAME
FRONT

FLAME
BACK

Fold

UP CUP

On first copy
Match A to B edges

On second copy
cut off A to C section
and remove tabs

Cut A Line

A

C B

BASE

DOWN CUP

Cut A Line

Match A to B edges

A

B

CANDLE CAP

Cut out
center
circle

WICK

Fold Tabs

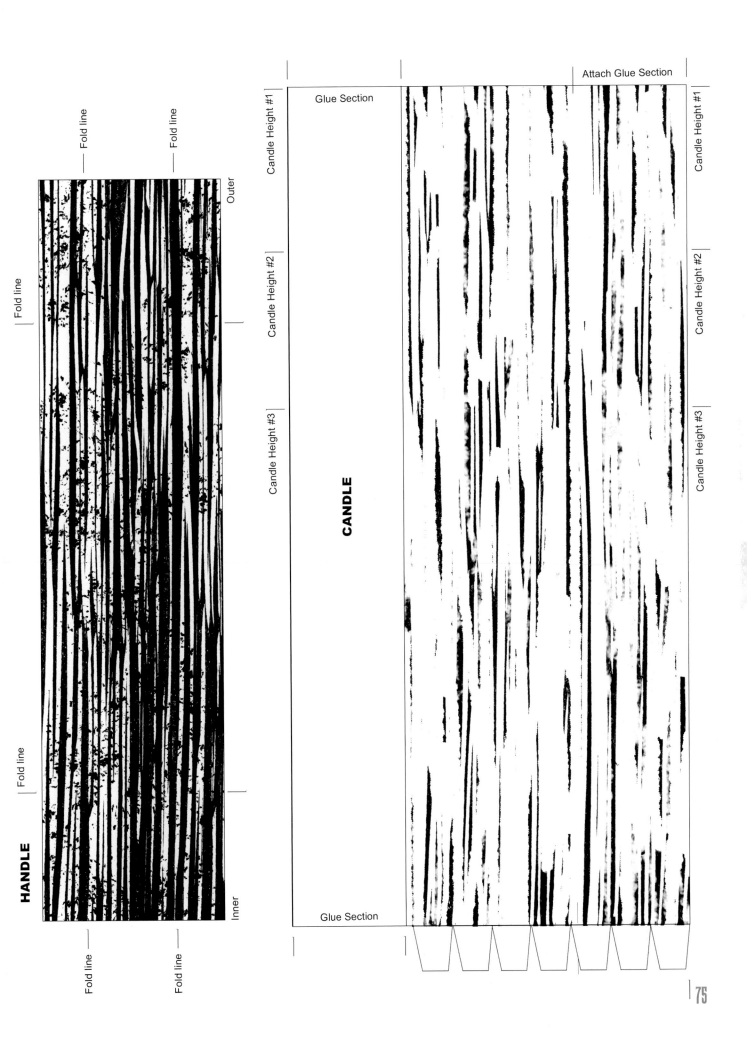

HANDLE

Fold line

Fold line

Fold line

Fold line

Fold line

Fold line

Outer

Inner

CANDLE

Glue Section

Attach Glue Section

Candle Height #1

Candle Height #2

Candle Height #3

Candle Height #1

Candle Height #2

Candle Height #3

Glue Section

Candlestick with Handle
Print Two Sheets

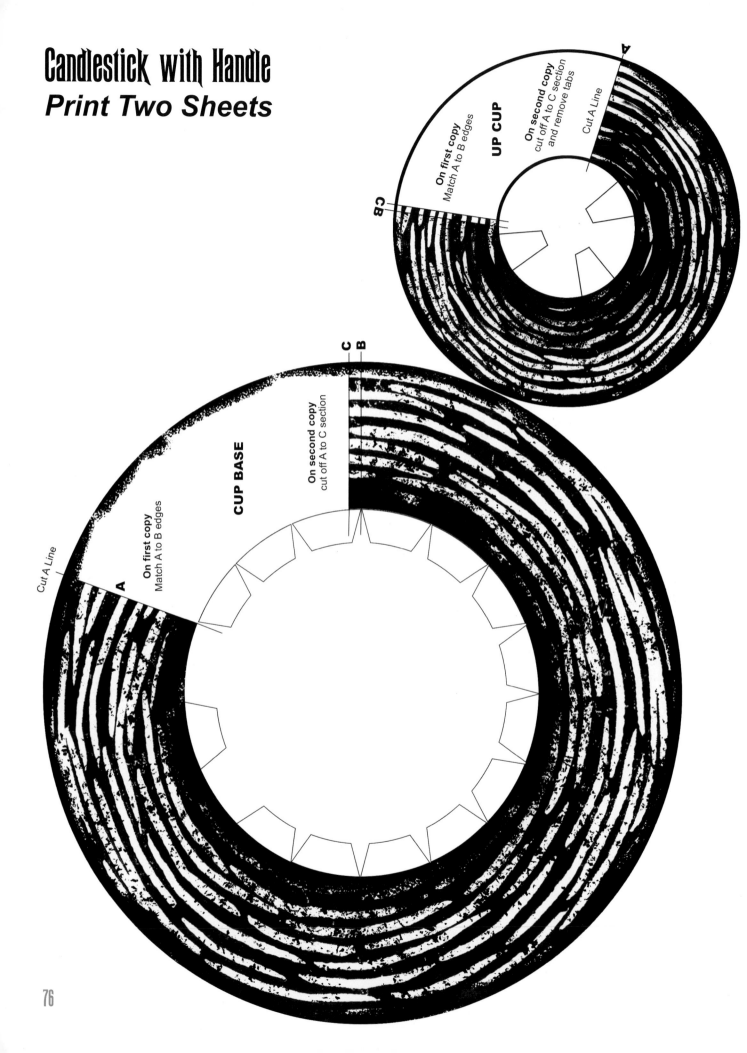

UP CUP

On first copy
Match A to B edges

On second copy
cut off A to C section
and remove tabs

Cut A Line

A

CB

CUP BASE

Cut A Line

A

On first copy
Match A to B edges

On second copy
cut off A to C section

Cut A Line

C
B

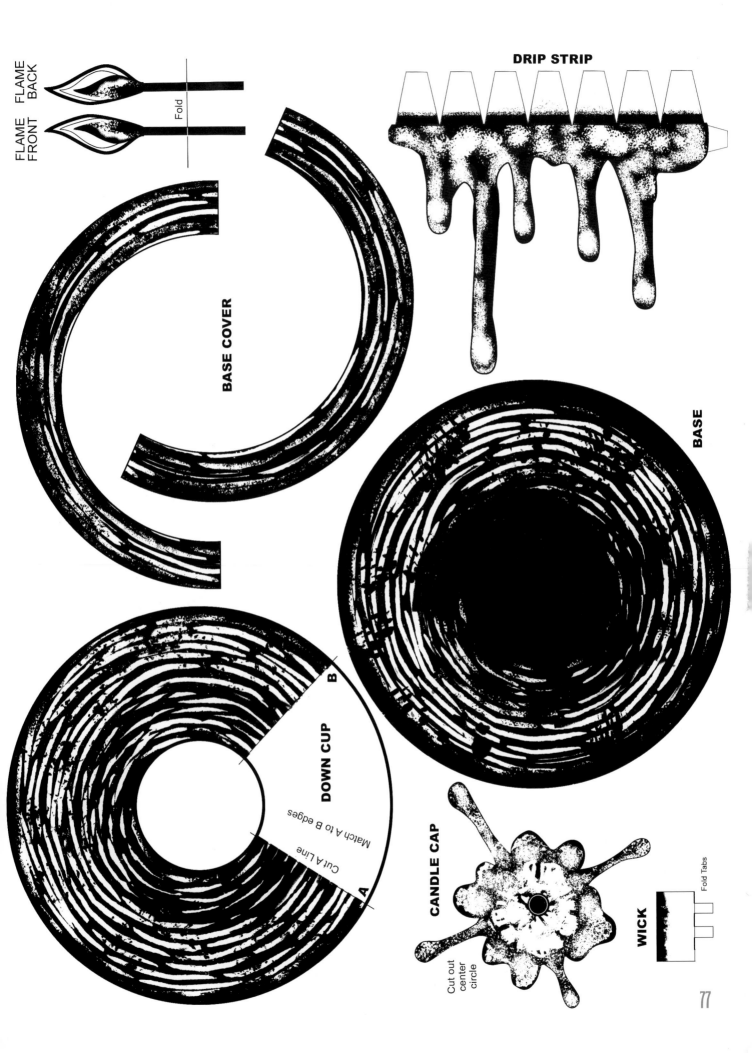

FLAME
FRONT

FLAME
BACK

Fold

DRIP STRIP

BASE COVER

BASE

DOWN CUP

Match A to B edges

Cut A Line

A

B

CANDLE CAP

Cut out
center
circle

WICK

Fold Tabs

77

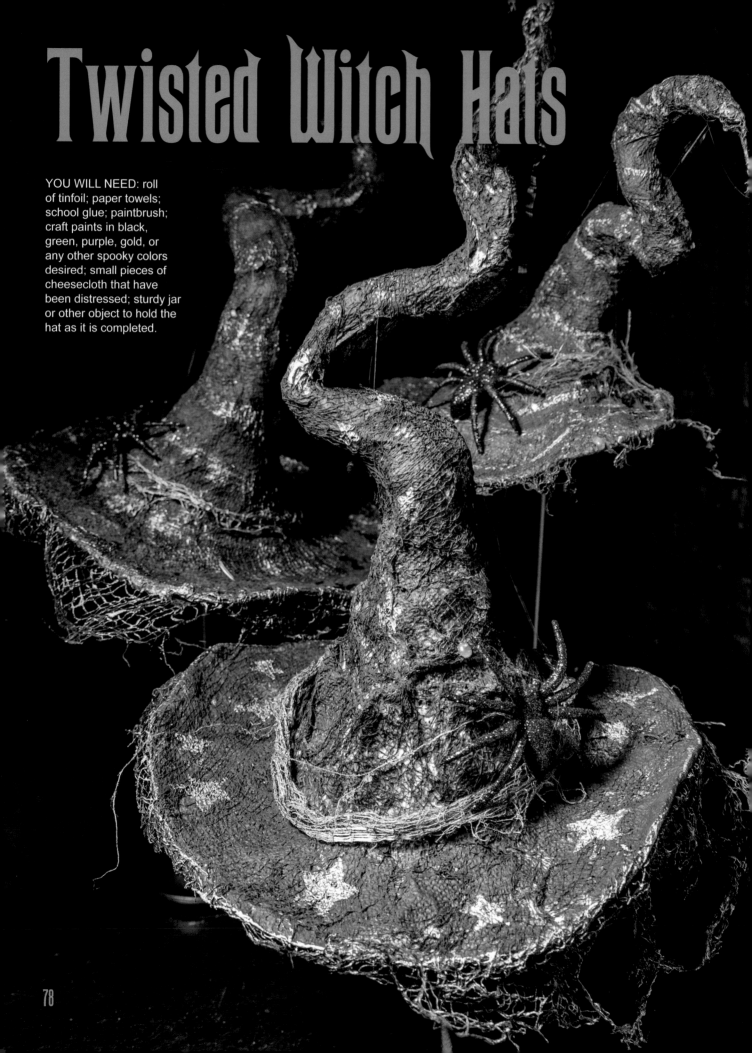

Twisted Witch Hats

YOU WILL NEED: roll of tinfoil; paper towels; school glue; paintbrush; craft paints in black, green, purple, gold, or any other spooky colors desired; small pieces of cheesecloth that have been distressed; sturdy jar or other object to hold the hat as it is completed.

twisted Hat shop

Display on candle holders

Some simple sketch ideas before beginning our sculpture.

If you have never sculpted before or been too afraid to try, this is a great introduction to creating something from nothing. One of the easiest shape-building materials is tinfoil. Crumple up a ball, and you have a starting point for many sculpture projects. Adding on more foil and crushing it together will create more bulk for even bigger forms. It can be bent, rolled, and flattened and still hold a shape. For this project, we will keep it small and simple and create a witch's hat.

1 With a sturdy jar on the table, tear off approximately a 10-inch piece of tinfoil. Press this down over the lid of a jar and form a tinfoil cap. This will be the inside rim of the hat.

The beginning of the hat base that will also form the inner rim of hat

Cheapest tinfoil will work just fine on this project. It will be covered with other materials.

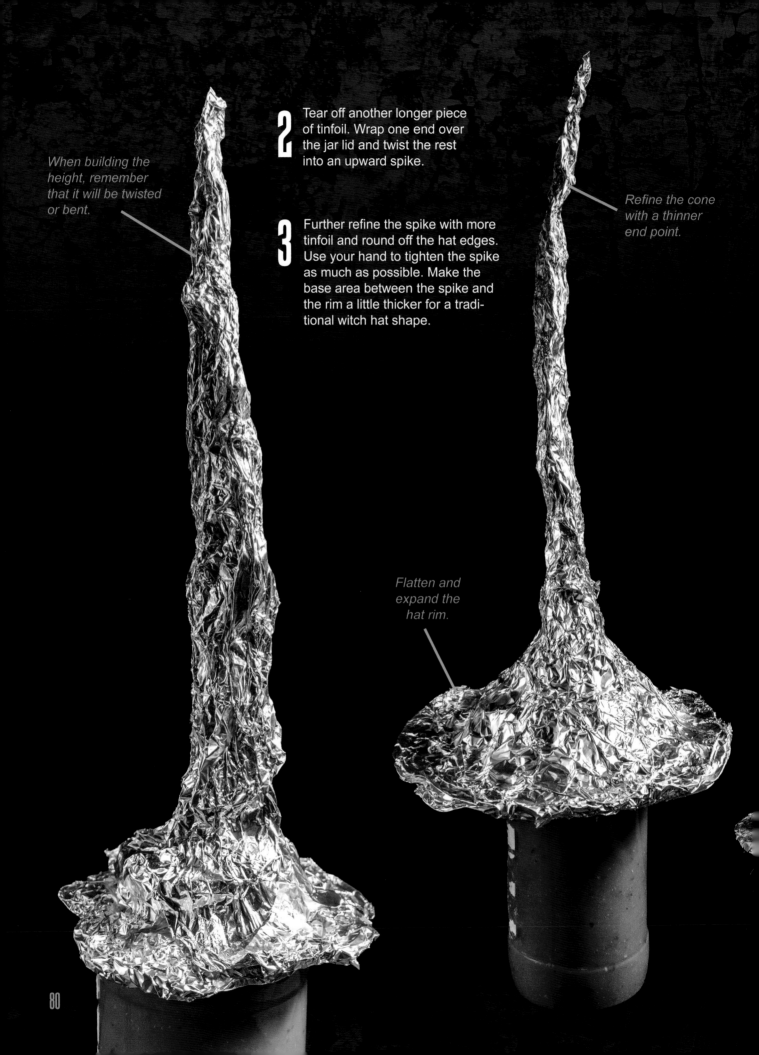

When building the height, remember that it will be twisted or bent.

2 Tear off another longer piece of tinfoil. Wrap one end over the jar lid and twist the rest into an upward spike.

3 Further refine the spike with more tinfoil and round off the hat edges. Use your hand to tighten the spike as much as possible. Make the base area between the spike and the rim a little thicker for a traditional witch hat shape.

Refine the cone with a thinner end point.

Flatten and expand the hat rim.

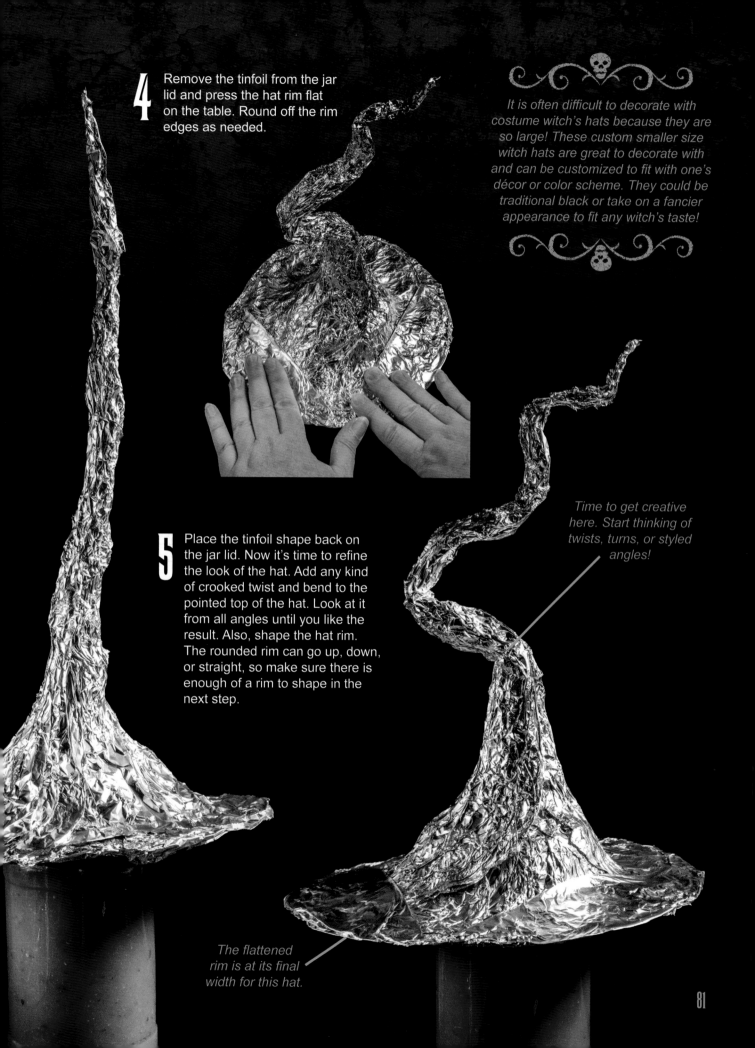

4 Remove the tinfoil from the jar lid and press the hat rim flat on the table. Round off the rim edges as needed.

It is often difficult to decorate with costume witch's hats because they are so large! These custom smaller size witch hats are great to decorate with and can be customized to fit with one's décor or color scheme. They could be traditional black or take on a fancier appearance to fit any witch's taste!

5 Place the tinfoil shape back on the jar lid. Now it's time to refine the look of the hat. Add any kind of crooked twist and bend to the pointed top of the hat. Look at it from all angles until you like the result. Also, shape the hat rim. The rounded rim can go up, down, or straight, so make sure there is enough of a rim to shape in the next step.

Time to get creative here. Start thinking of twists, turns, or styled angles!

The flattened rim is at its final width for this hat.

81

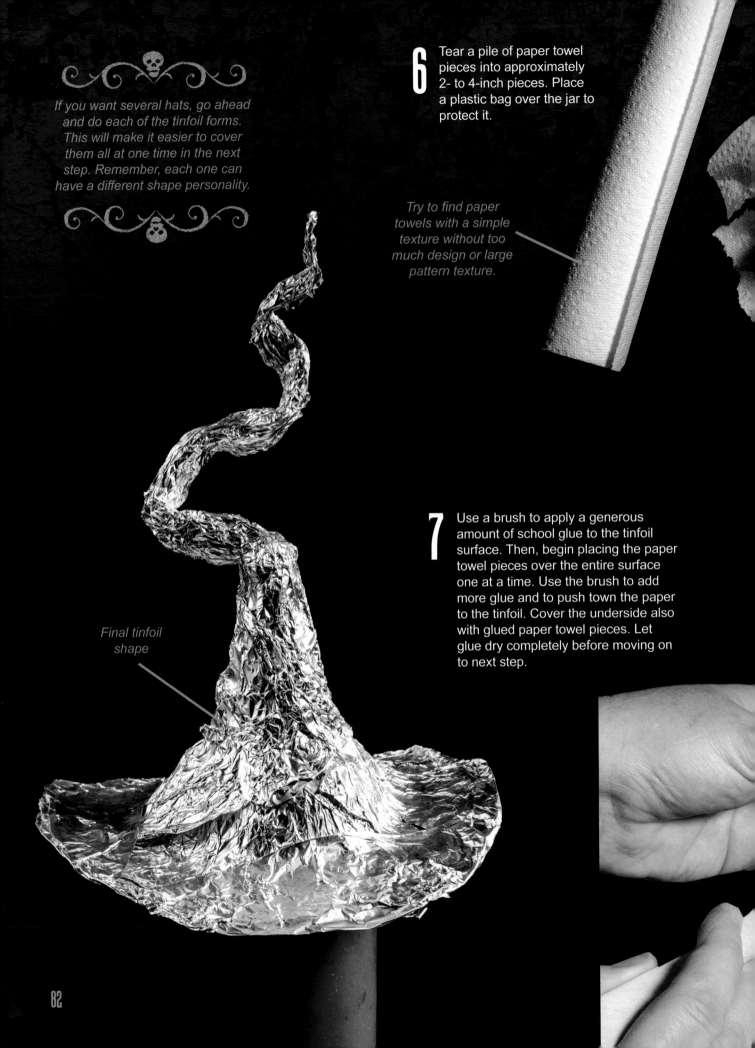

If you want several hats, go ahead and do each of the tinfoil forms. This will make it easier to cover them all at one time in the next step. Remember, each one can have a different shape personality.

6 Tear a pile of paper towel pieces into approximately 2- to 4-inch pieces. Place a plastic bag over the jar to protect it.

Try to find paper towels with a simple texture without too much design or large pattern texture.

7 Use a brush to apply a generous amount of school glue to the tinfoil surface. Then, begin placing the paper towel pieces over the entire surface one at a time. Use the brush to add more glue and to push town the paper to the tinfoil. Cover the underside also with glued paper towel pieces. Let glue dry completely before moving on to next step.

Final tinfoil shape

Let this glue step dry overnight.

Add some glue to the tinfoil surface before applying the paper towel pieces.

Use plastic bag over the jar to protect it.

The inner hat rim will help it to sit on a stand, if needed. The inner rim can be small or large.

Experiment with adding a bit of a ruffle detail around the center.

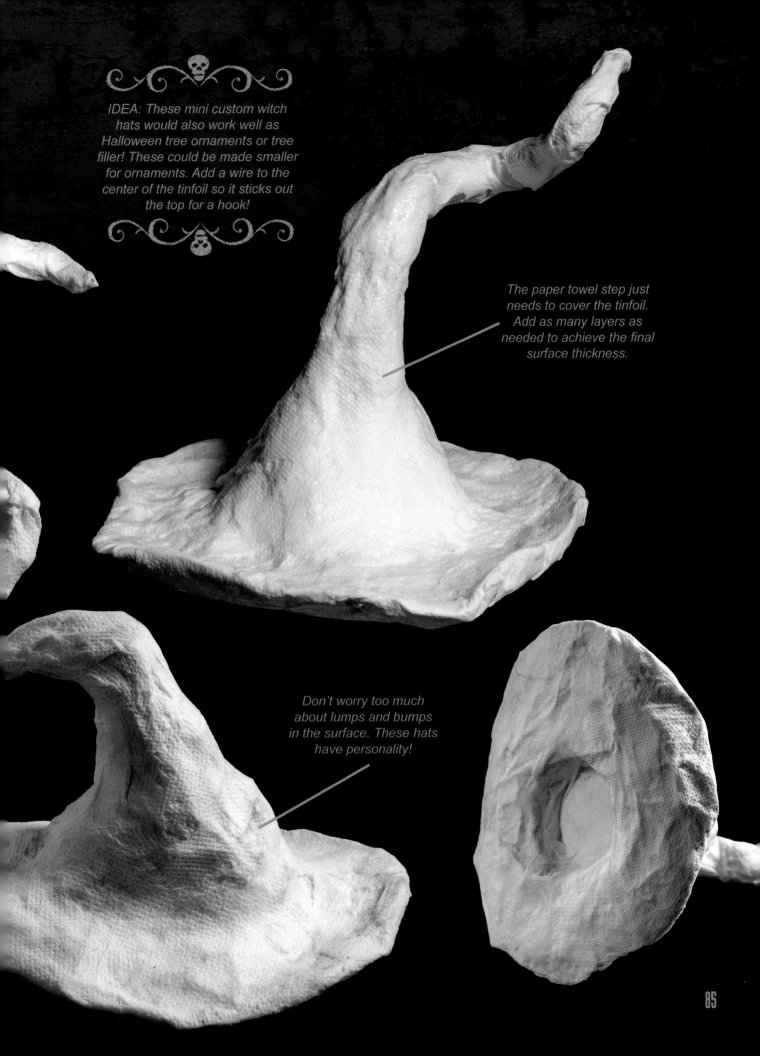

IDEA: These mini custom witch hats would also work well as Halloween tree ornaments or tree filler! These could be made smaller for ornaments. Add a wire to the center of the tinfoil so it sticks out the top for a hook!

The paper towel step just needs to cover the tinfoil. Add as many layers as needed to achieve the final surface thickness.

Don't worry too much about lumps and bumps in the surface. These hats have personality!

85

8 Cut several 4- to 6-inch pieces of cheese-cloth. Use fingers to loosen the weave and fray the edges. Remove the hat from jar and glue the underside of the hat. Place pieces of cheesecloth over the glue and use a brush to push down into the surface. Each cheesecloth piece should overlap slightly. Fabric pieces can extend off the edges as shown.

The cheesecloth loose "hairs" create an amazing detail on the final hats. Be sure to get some glue on them to stiffen them!

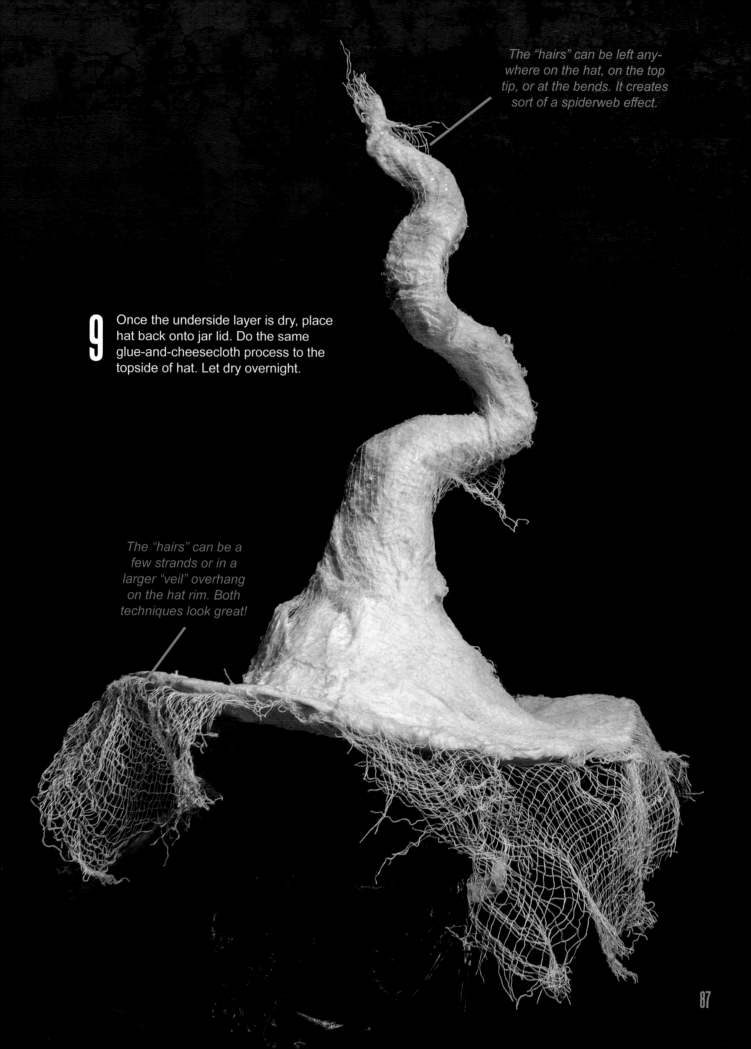

*The "hairs" can be left any-
where on the hat, on the top
tip, or at the bends. It creates
sort of a spiderweb effect.*

9 Once the underside layer is dry, place
hat back onto jar lid. Do the same
glue-and-cheesecloth process to the
topside of hat. Let dry overnight.

*The "hairs" can be a
few strands or in a
larger "veil" overhang
on the hat rim. Both
techniques look great!*

10 Using a chip brush, paint the hat with black craft paint, including the fabric hanging off the rim of the hat. Some of the white can still show through for a rougher, worn appearance or be filled in completely. Let dry completely.

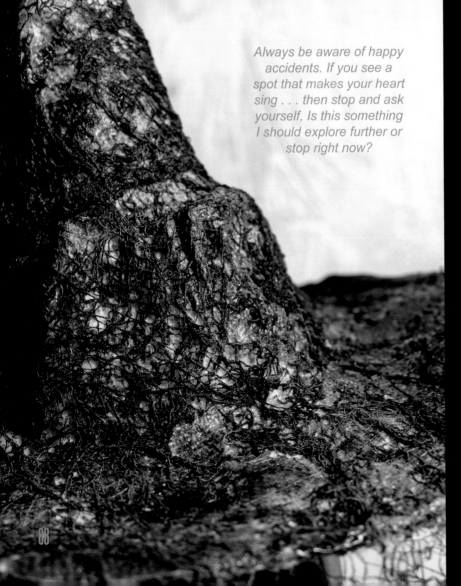

Always be aware of happy accidents. If you see a spot that makes your heart sing . . . then stop and ask yourself, Is this something I should explore further or stop right now?

TECHNIQUE IDEA: This paint stage has a spooky vibe already. If this is a look that will work in your theme, call it done!

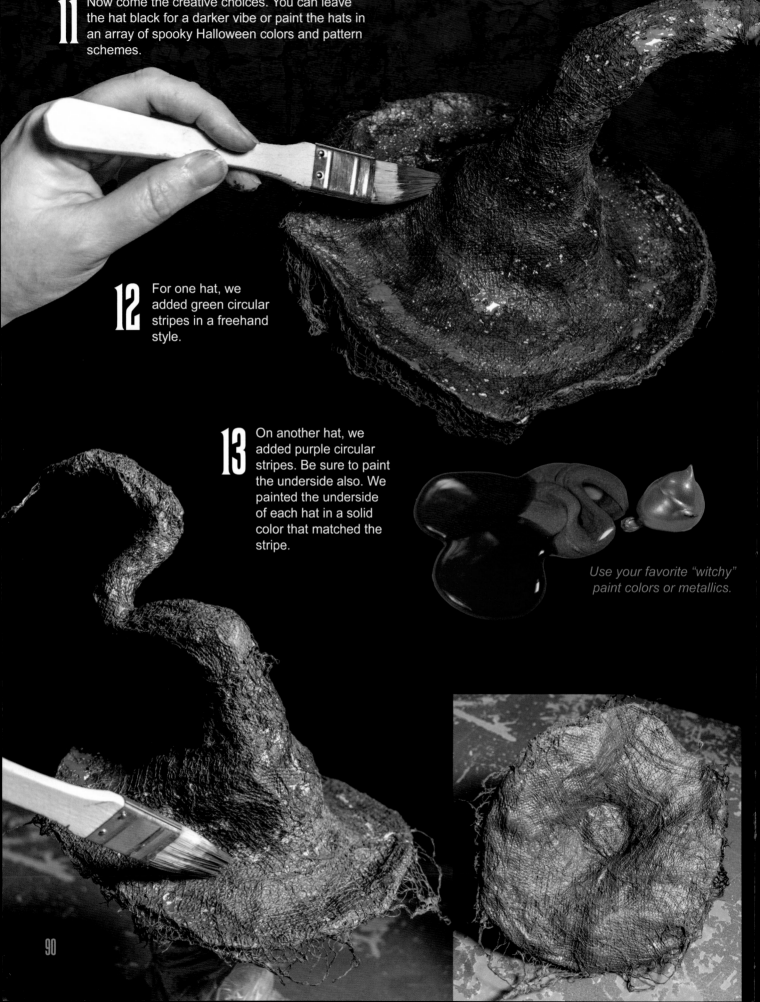

11 Now come the creative choices. You can leave the hat black for a darker vibe or paint the hats in an array of spooky Halloween colors and pattern schemes.

12 For one hat, we added green circular stripes in a freehand style.

13 On another hat, we added purple circular stripes. Be sure to paint the underside also. We painted the underside of each hat in a solid color that matched the stripe.

Use your favorite "witchy" paint colors or metallics.

Easy masking tape stencil

14 For our third hat, we made a stencil by covering a piece of paper with masking tape, then drew a few star sizes and cut out with a utility knife. Place the template over the hat and use a brush to stamp paint into the open star shape at various points on the hat with gold paint. Dry brush the hat rim and edge fabric in the same gold paint.

15 Since the gold looked so good on the star hat, we used a wide brush to add some gold circles on the green hat.

16 On the purple hat, we used a detail brush to add some smaller lines in gold for just the right amount of bling.

17 Paint a strip of cheesecloth for each of the hats to use as the hatbands. Just add a touch of purple or gold paint. We went with the very worn look on these, so the loose threads and stray ends were perfect. Once dry, drape each hatband around the center and add a loose knot to hold in place.

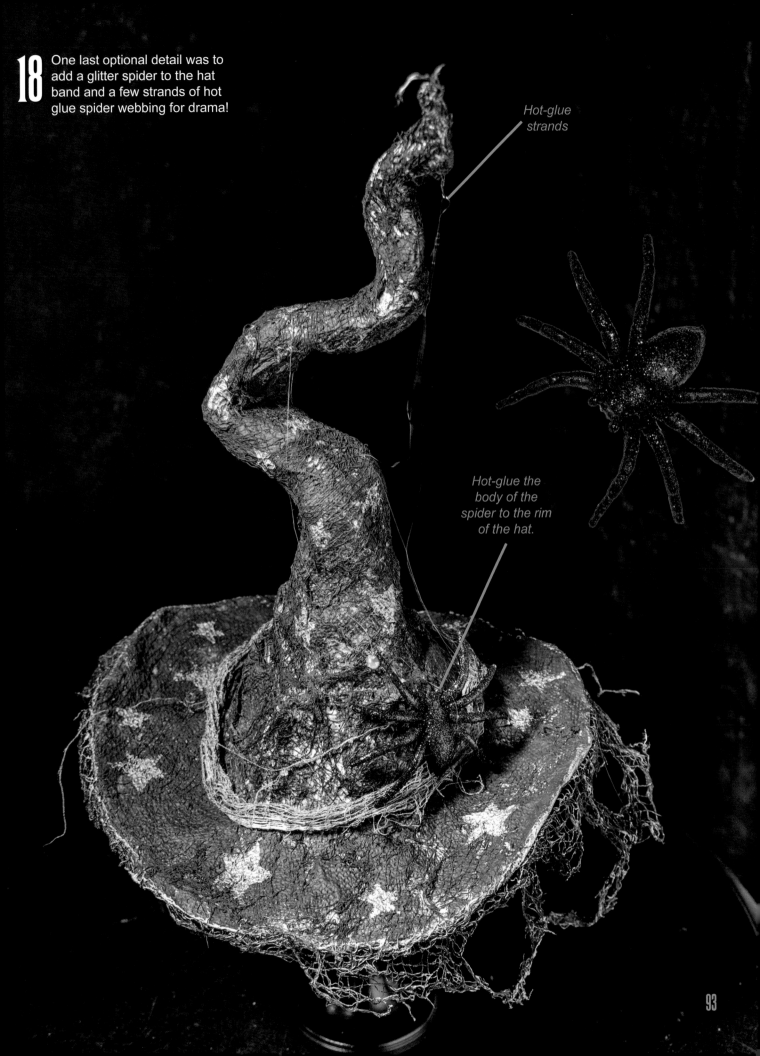

18 One last optional detail was to add a glitter spider to the hat band and a few strands of hot glue spider webbing for drama!

Hot-glue strands

Hot-glue the body of the spider to the rim of the hat.

*A FEW IDEAS to display these hats:
Add hats to the tops of tall candlesticks to showcase the hats as if in
a shop. Add a wire sticking out of a
flower arrangement to have the hats
floating above or as a centerpiece
for a Halloween table.*

Grab the cauldron, kick up the broom, it's time to put on your hat ...and zoom!

Final twisted hat ready to be displayed for Halloween!

Halloween Daguerreotypes

Spooky Portrait Keepsakes

YOU WILL NEED: black matte board *(or black illustration board, which is black all the way through the material)*, ruler, blue & white colored pencil, X-acto knife with extra blades, Tacky Glue, low-temperature hot glue & hot-glue gun, Super Glue, black craft paint, straight-cut wooden craft sticks, small hinges *(1-inch length)*, Tim Holtz metallic photo frames *(pack comes with 6 frames in two sizes)* or create your own miniature photo frames cut out of matte board and painted gold, ½ yard of faux red velvet fabric, gold washi tape or metallic gold paint, ballpoint pen, prints of small Halloween costume photos.

These metallic photo frames by Tim Holtz caught our creative eye when we saw them. We knew instantly that they would make great, custom daguerreotype picture frames with just a bit of work. If you collect old daguerreotypes, you know they can be pricey and often come with an old photo already in them. We wanted to make our own and show off our little monster family in the best possible way!

Metallic Matte

Should you not be able to find Tim Holtz's metallic photo frame packs . . . *don't panic!* Here is an alternative, hand-made metallic matte method.

1

Cut out a 2.5 x 3-inch board from illustration or matte board. Draw a center frame shape of choice.

2

Use utility knife to cut out center.

3

Use ballpoint pen to press firmly a simple design around edges.

4

Use metallic gold paint to cover the matte. Let dry.

5

The final painted photo matte

Tim Holtz metallic photo frames

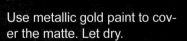

Building the Matte Holder

1 Use X-acto knife to cut craft sticks down to fit around one of the metallic photo frames. Leave a 1/16-inch space between the wood and the frame all the way around. This extra space will be for the fabric to fit into for the next step. Two of the wood sides should overlap at the ends of the adjoining sticks so they will form a tight corner. Use low-temperature hot glue to join the corners. Press down the glue if it gets too thick, or trim with a knife once it is cool.

1/8-inch width wooden craft sticks

Top edge overlaps the vertical side piece

Completed wooden frame that will hold the metallic matte

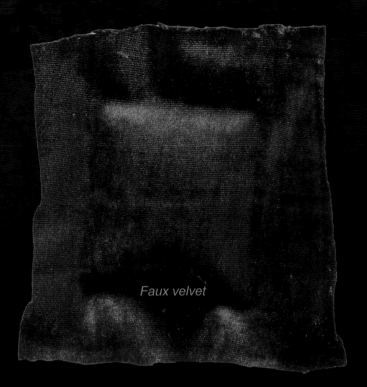

Faux velvet

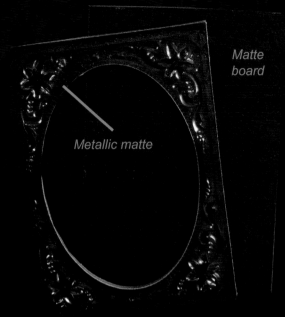

Matte board

Metallic matte

2 Cut out a matching size piece of matte board to the size of the metallic frame. Set aside. Cut a piece of faux velvet the size of wood frame, with 1-inch left all the way around. Add Tacky Glue to each of the interior sides of the wood frame, spreading out the glue to cover these sides fully. Lay the fabric over the frame. Add Tacky Glue to back of cut matte board, then press this board inside the wood frame over the velvet to hold in place. Use scissors to make an angled cut at each of the fabric corners, as shown. Let dry at least ten minutes.

Velvet pulled tight to wooden frame to backside

Matte board pressed over velvet and inside wooden frame

3 Turn the frame over to the backside. Run a bead of glue along one side of the wood frame and pull the fabric over and toward the backside. Make sure the outer wood edge fabric lies flat as possible. Do the same on the opposite sides.

Cut velvet corners angled toward frame

4 Trim off excess fabric at the corners. Getting the corners to lie as flat as possible is the trickiest part. Use your finger to press on each glued corner to help keep it down as it dries. Do one side at a time, letting each side dry ten minutes before moving on to the next side.

5 Test fit the metallic frame over the matte board but do not glue in place.

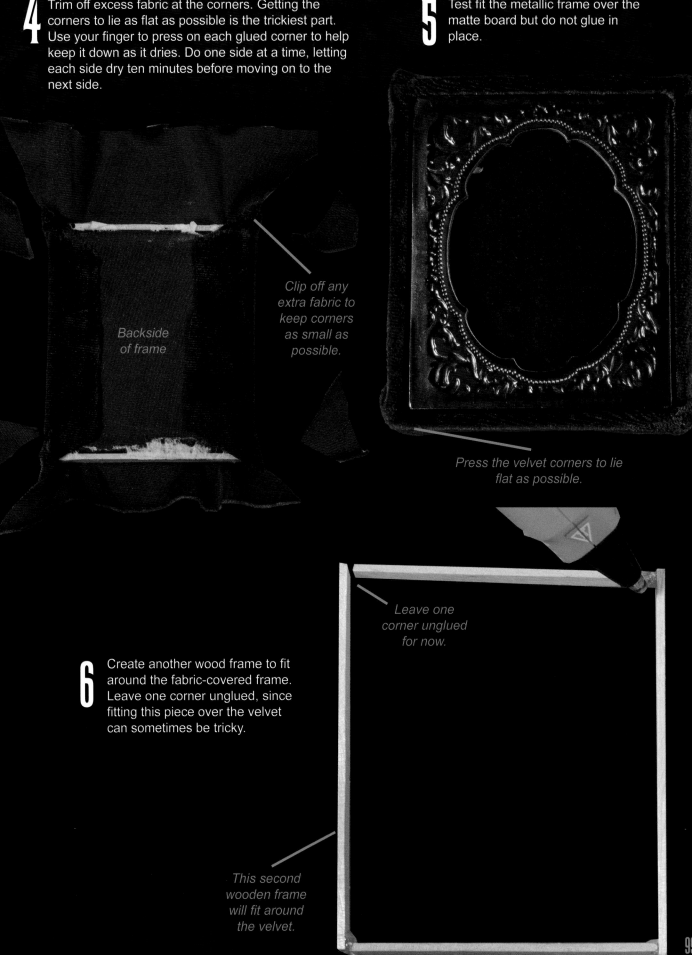

Clip off any extra fabric to keep corners as small as possible.

Backside of frame

Press the velvet corners to lie flat as possible.

Leave one corner unglued for now.

6 Create another wood frame to fit around the fabric-covered frame. Leave one corner unglued, since fitting this piece over the velvet can sometimes be tricky.

This second wooden frame will fit around the velvet.

7 This frame needs to have a bit of gold shine. Use either gold washi tape or gold metallic paint. Bend piece of washi tape over the top edges of the frame. It doesn't have to cover the bottom edge, since it will be hidden. Or paint the frame with metallic gold paint and let dry.

Only the top edge of gold will show in final.

Gold washi tape

Washi Tape

Gold Paint

folkArt
TRUSTED QUALITY
Enamels
4129E METALLIC GOLD
SUPERIOR COVERAGE
GLOSS FINISH
ACRYLIC PAINT
DISHWASHER SAFE

8 Wrap this gold frame around the velvet sides, holding it tight to the inner frame, and hot-glue the last corner to hold it in place.

9 Measure the wood frame's outer size from the previous step. Cut a matte board to fit this measurement and use as a frame base. Cut ⅜-inch strips to fit the sides. Make two of the sides ²⁄₁₆-inch longer so they can tightly fit together.

10 Tape the side pieces to the base with masking tape on the interior.

11 Fold up the sides and add a small amount of hot glue to the interior corners. Hot-glue any seams on the back that have gaps.

The interior base matte dimensions come from the width and height of the wood and velvet piece in previous step.

⅜-inch-deep sides

Top and bottom pieces are ²⁄₁₆-inch longer than interior width.

Keep the masking tape toward the bottom so it won't show in the final.

Final frame container

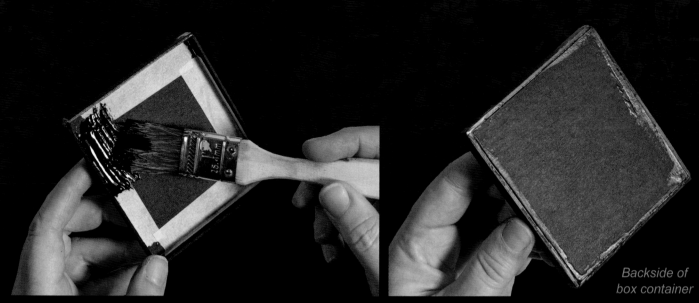

Backside of box container

12 Paint both the inside and outside of the box with black craft paint. Let dry. Insert the rest of the assembled frame into this box.

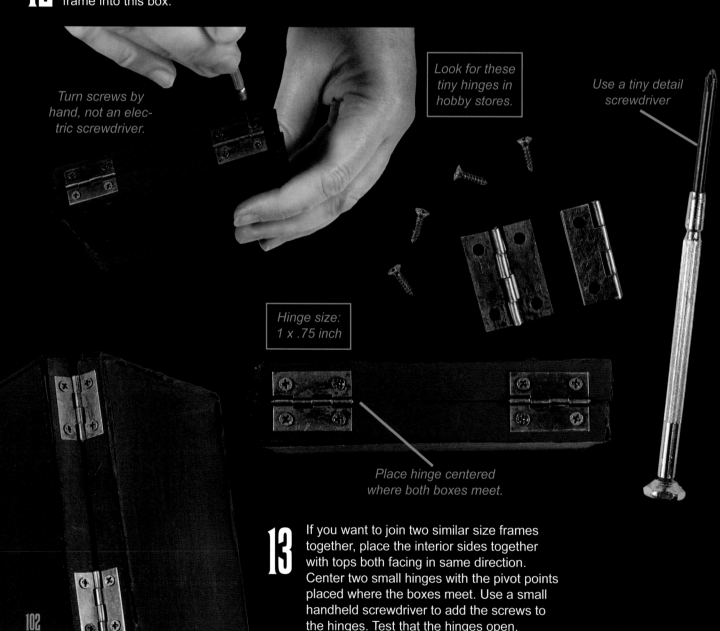

Turn screws by hand, not an electric screwdriver.

Look for these tiny hinges in hobby stores.

Use a tiny detail screwdriver

Hinge size: 1 x .75 inch

Place hinge centered where both boxes meet.

13 If you want to join two similar size frames together, place the interior sides together with tops both facing in same direction. Center two small hinges with the pivot points placed where the boxes meet. Use a small handheld screwdriver to add the screws to the hinges. Test that the hinges open.

14

Once photos have been inserted, use small amount of su-perglue on each of the metallic frame corners to secure.

These Halloween daguerreotypes frames look great grouped together on a table or mantle.

Daguerreotypes can be joined with a hinge or left singular. The singular frames should be able to stand up on their own.

*TIP: Use **Tintype** phone app to take cool black-and-white photos with an aged appearance. Use a photo editing program to size several photos down to fit these frame sizes and group them together on an 8x10 sheet size. Print this file on photo paper on a home printer or send off to be printed professionally. Cut out all the photos and add to the frames.*

Freaky Frames

YOU WILL NEED: several black foam core boards *(Look for the boards that have the black interior foam. It will save time in the painting stage later.)*, matte board (or similar weight board), ruler, blue & white colored pencil, X-acto knife with extra blades, Tacky Glue, craft paints (black, brown, red), popsicle sticks, thin craft wire, small picture frame hooks, variety of photo mattes *(we used Tim Holtz mattes),* prints of small, Halloween costume photos

Simple Stack & Strips Frame

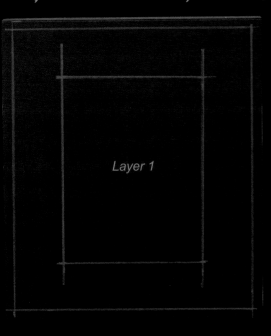

Layer 1

Layer 2

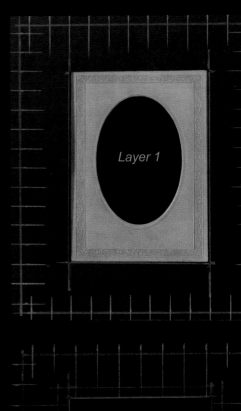

Layer 1

Layer 2

1 Measure 1.5 inches from each edge of matte frame onto black foam core board. Trace around the matte frame or photo size needed. Cut out this first layer, using an X-acto knife. Also, cut out the space where the matte frame will fit. Mark ¼-inch in from all outer sides, using blue colored pencil.

The template for this frame is on page 112.

2 Using a white colored pencil, mark every ½-inch along all sides. If the side measurement does not equal to the ½-inch, divide the remaining space equally to each of the ends of that side. So, if there is ⅛-inch left over, add 1/16-inch extra to both left and right ends.

3 Measure from side to side the blue marked lines of first layer to get second foam board layer dimensions. Cut out using X-acto knife. The inner cut edge will overlap first layer's inner cut edge to hold the matte frame *(or photo)* in place. Using the blue pencil, mark ¼-inch on outer and inner edges. Use white pencil to repeat *step 2* on this layer for both inner and outer

The Tramp Art frames of the 1900s were the inspiration for these frames. The original Tramp Art frames were carved out of recycled wood from cigar boxes or shipping crates and are highly sought after by collectors. Our version achieves the same handcrafted look but uses foam core boards stacked in layers and cut out with a utility knife.

Several design templates are provided, but one could come up with all sorts of designs inspired by traditional Tramp Art frames. Do an internet search to see what different shapes and designs were created, and create your own designs. Once the measurements have been drawn out and the cuts mastered, one could create three or more frames in a single weekend.

4 On this frame, the third layer uses individual cut strips with some space left at the meeting points of each strip. Mark each of these pieces with the blue ¼-inch margins, and the white ½-inch spacing.

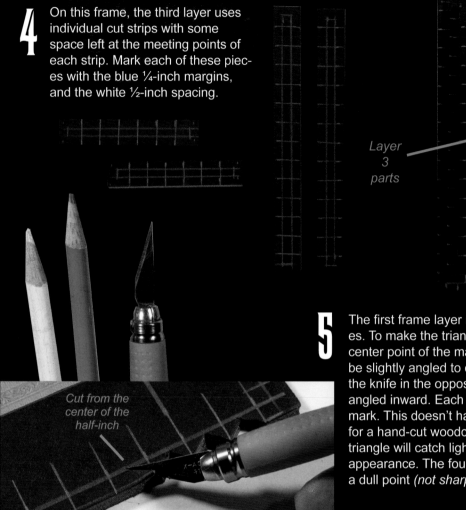

Layer 3 parts

5 The first frame layer is triangle-cut only on the outer edges. To make the triangle cuts, place the X-acto knife at the center point of the marked ½-inch area. The blade should be slightly angled to create an inward-facing bevel. Rotate the knife in the opposite direction for the second cut, also angled inward. Each cut should stop at the white ½-inch mark. This doesn't have to be perfect. The look is aiming for a hand-cut woodcarved effect. The bevel created on the triangle will catch light and add to the overall dimensional appearance. The four outer corners can be left with a dull point *(not sharp)* or made into a flat pointed wedge.

Cut from the center of the half-inch

The ends will stop at the half-inch marks.

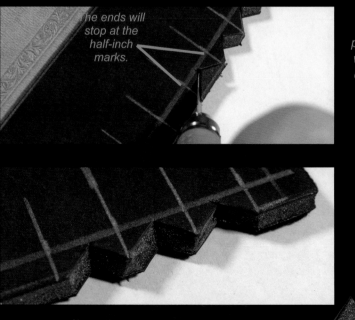

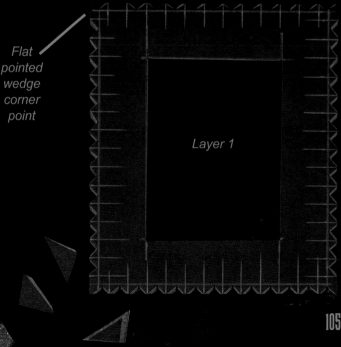

Flat pointed wedge corner point

Layer 1

Outer edges

6 Do the same triangle cuts for the second layer on both the inner and outer edges.

7 The third layer strips also get cut on both long sides, with the ends creating a rough point. Stack all the layers in place between the blue-marked ¼-inch borders. Tacky glue each layer, making sure the pieces are centered and straight between the blue-marked lines. Let dry.

8 See "Painting the Frames," on pages 122–127.

Glue layers into place between the blue-marked lines.

Aleene's
ORIGINAL

ORIGINAL
TACKY
GLUE

⅛ Favorite
GLUE

asive

OZ (473 mL)

The foam core board cuts easily with a sharp blade. If it begins tearing the foam board, put in a new blade.

Four-Corner Squares Frame

The template for this frame is on page 113.

1 Print out the *Four-Corner Squares Frame* template. Cut out along the outer edges. Use pencil to trace out the pattern on to the foam core board. Use the X-acto knife to poke a mark at each of the matte board corners and then use a pencil to make these connecting lines.

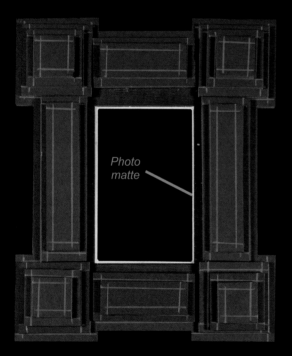

Photo matte

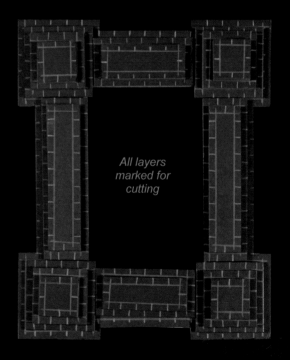

All layers marked for cutting

2 Each color on the template represents a frame layer. The bold lines are *layer 1* and will hold the photo or photo matte. The next color line in will be *layer 2,* and so forth. Trace each template layer onto the foam core board and cut out.

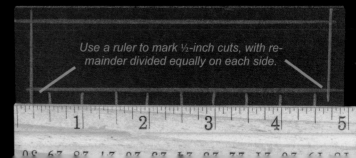

Use a ruler to mark ½-inch cuts, with remainder divided equally on each side.

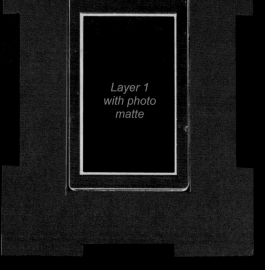

3 Cut the first layer from template. The photo matte board should fit inside the center rectangle.

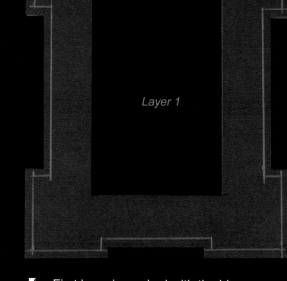

4 First layer is marked with the blue pencil for the ¼-inch margins on the outside only.

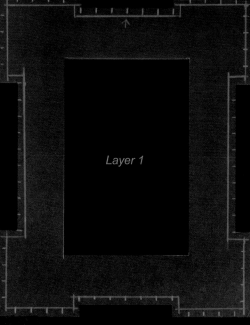

5 First layer is marked with the white pencil on the entire ½-inch cut mark lines.

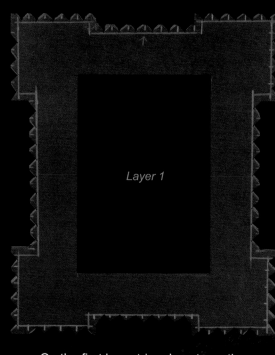

6 On the first layer triangle cuts, notice that the corners have been left with an uncut triangle. If you make end points too fine or small, they will break easily, so we left flat pointed wedge corners.

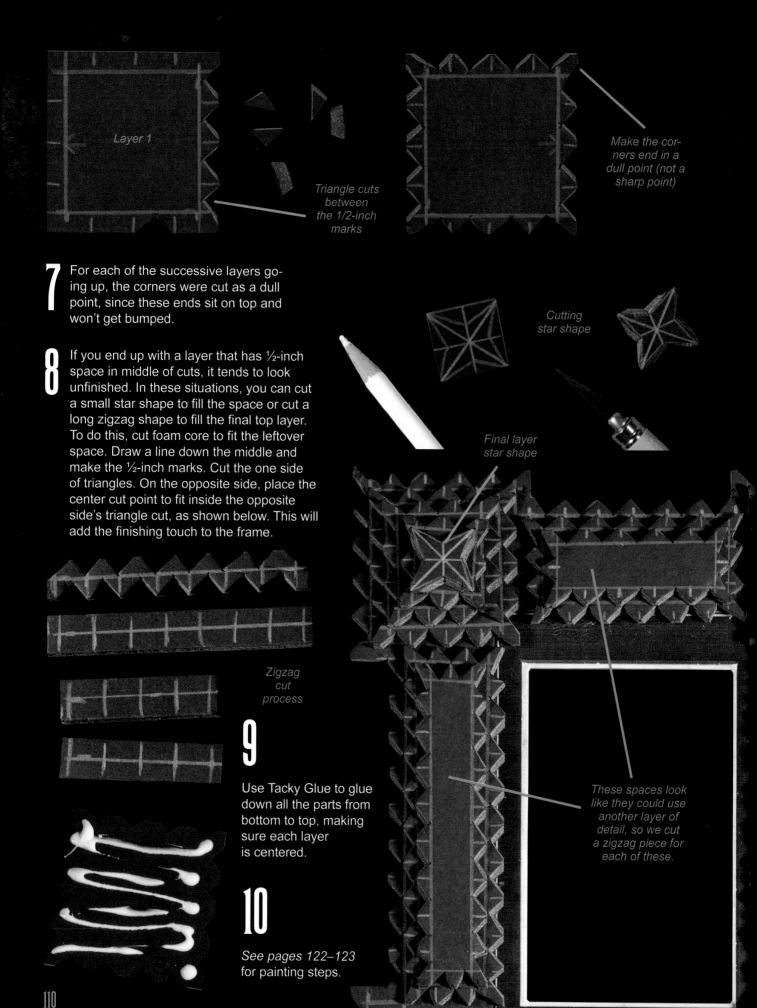

Layer 1

Triangle cuts between the 1/2-inch marks

Make the corners end in a dull point (not a sharp point)

7 For each of the successive layers going up, the corners were cut as a dull point, since these ends sit on top and won't get bumped.

8 If you end up with a layer that has ½-inch space in middle of cuts, it tends to look unfinished. In these situations, you can cut a small star shape to fill the space or cut a long zigzag shape to fill the final top layer. To do this, cut foam core to fit the leftover space. Draw a line down the middle and make the ½-inch marks. Cut the one side of triangles. On the opposite side, place the center cut point to fit inside the opposite side's triangle cut, as shown below. This will add the finishing touch to the frame.

Cutting star shape

Final layer star shape

Zigzag cut process

9 Use Tacky Glue to glue down all the parts from bottom to top, making sure each layer is centered.

10 *See pages 122–123 for painting steps.*

These spaces look like they could use another layer of detail, so we cut a zigzag piece for each of these.

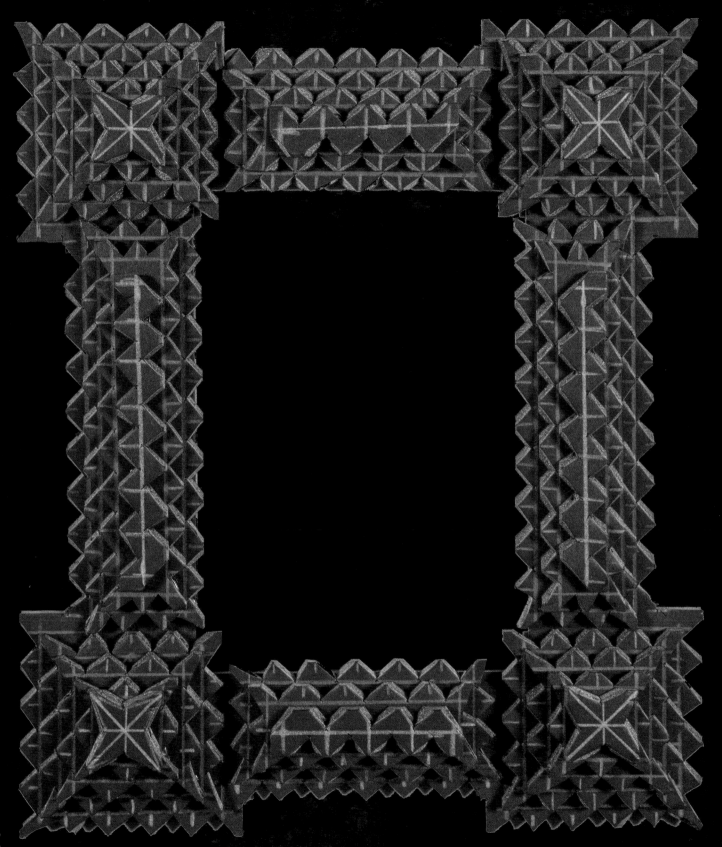

*Final parts for the Four-
Corner Square Frame*

Simple Stack and Strips Frame

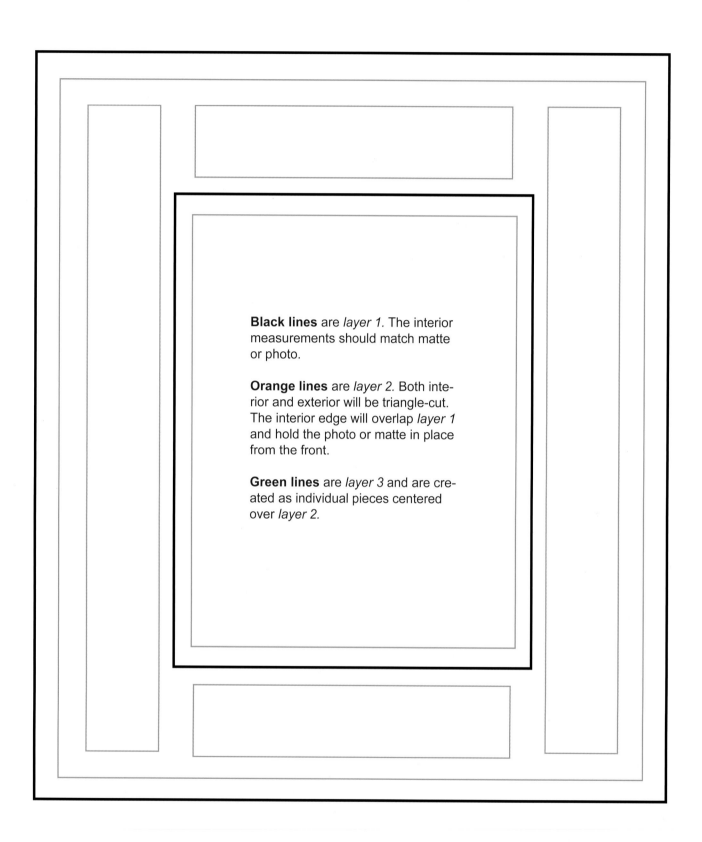

Black lines are *layer 1.* The interior measurements should match matte or photo.

Orange lines are *layer 2.* Both interior and exterior will be triangle-cut. The interior edge will overlap *layer 1* and hold the photo or matte in place from the front.

Green lines are *layer 3* and are created as individual pieces centered over *layer 2.*

Four-Corners Frame

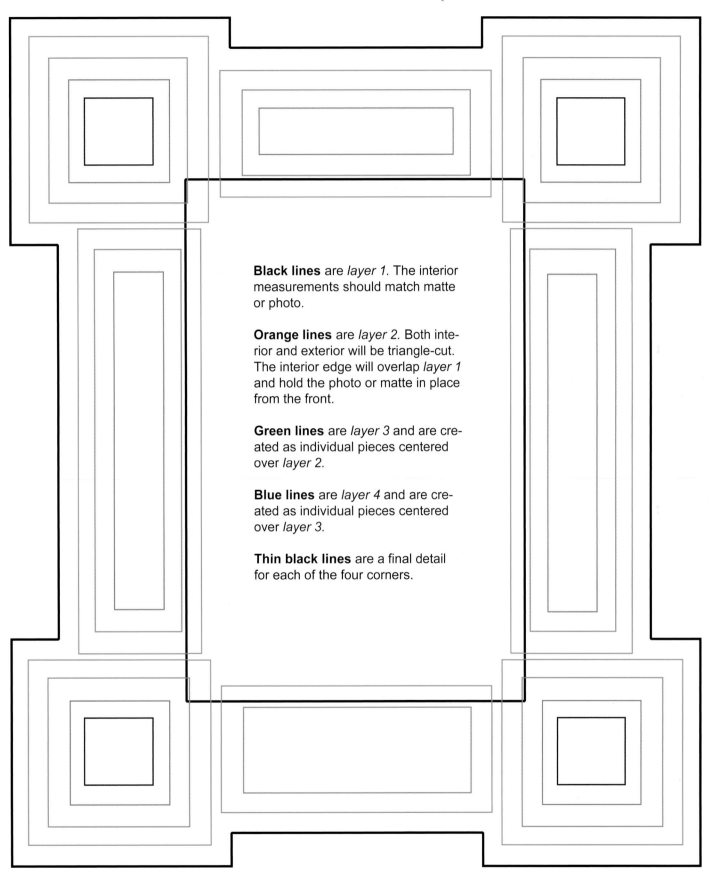

Black lines are *layer 1.* The interior measurements should match matte or photo.

Orange lines are *layer 2.* Both interior and exterior will be triangle-cut. The interior edge will overlap *layer 1* and hold the photo or matte in place from the front.

Green lines are *layer 3* and are created as individual pieces centered over *layer 2.*

Blue lines are *layer 4* and are created as individual pieces centered over *layer 3.*

Thin black lines are a final detail for each of the four corners.

Cat's-Ears Frame

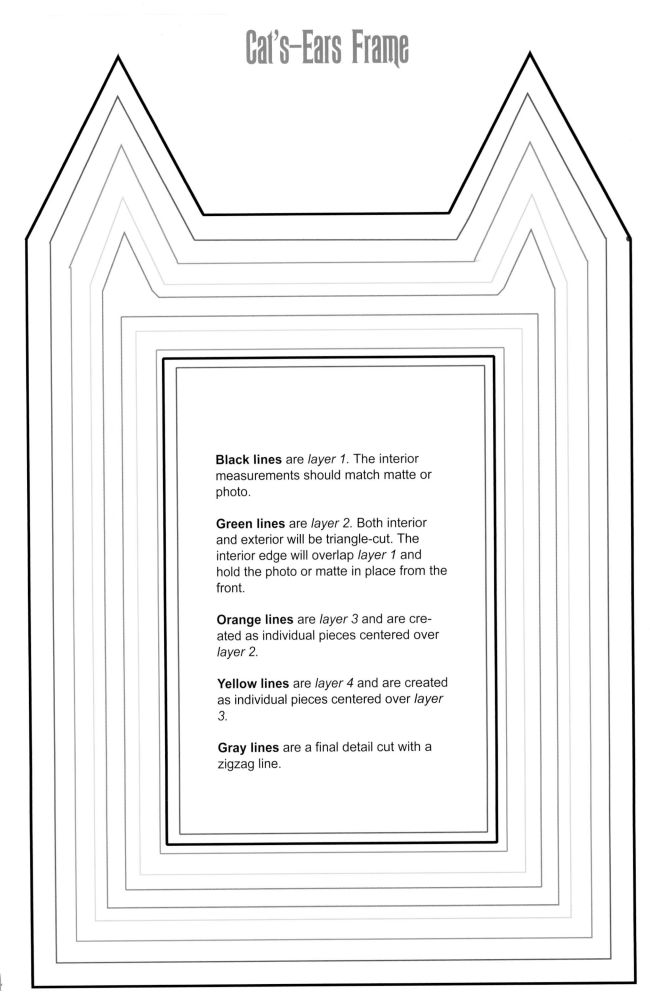

Black lines are *layer 1.* The interior measurements should match matte or photo.

Green lines are *layer 2.* Both interior and exterior will be triangle-cut. The interior edge will overlap *layer 1* and hold the photo or matte in place from the front.

Orange lines are *layer 3* and are created as individual pieces centered over *layer 2.*

Yellow lines are *layer 4* and are created as individual pieces centered over *layer 3.*

Gray lines are a final detail cut with a zigzag line.

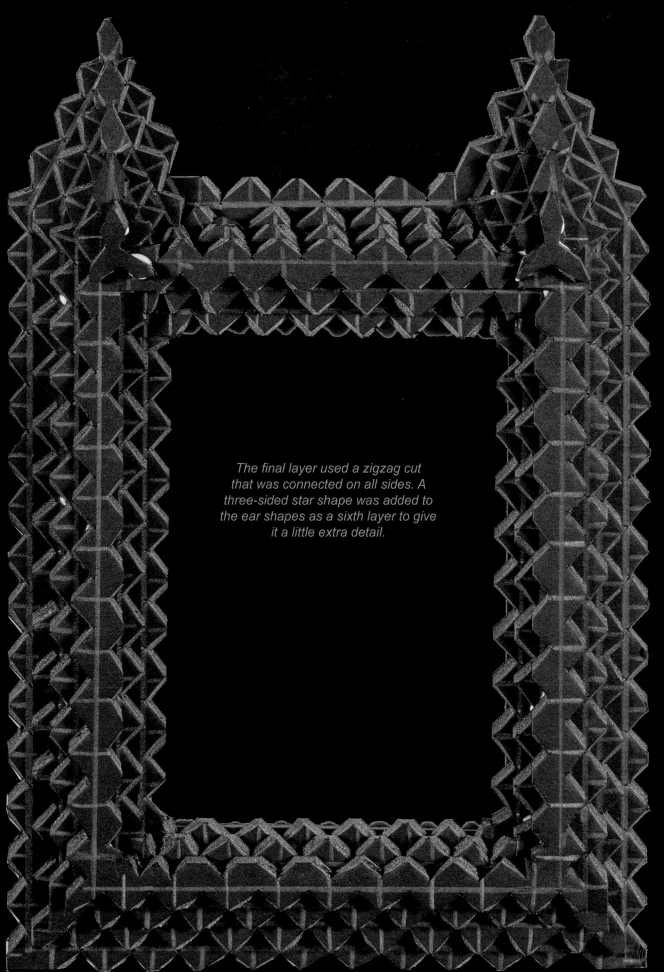

The final layer used a zigzag cut that was connected on all sides. A three-sided star shape was added to the ear shapes as a sixth layer to give it a little extra detail.

Double Frame

Black lines are *layer 1.* The interior measurements should match matte or photo.

Orange lines are *layer 2.* Both interior and exterior will be triangle-cut. The interior edge will overlap *layer 1* and hold the photo or matte in place from the front.

Green lines are *layer 3* and are created as individual pieces centered over *layer 2.*

Light Green *layer 4* sits on *layer 1* toward the center.

Blue lines sit on the light green layer as a zigzag cut.

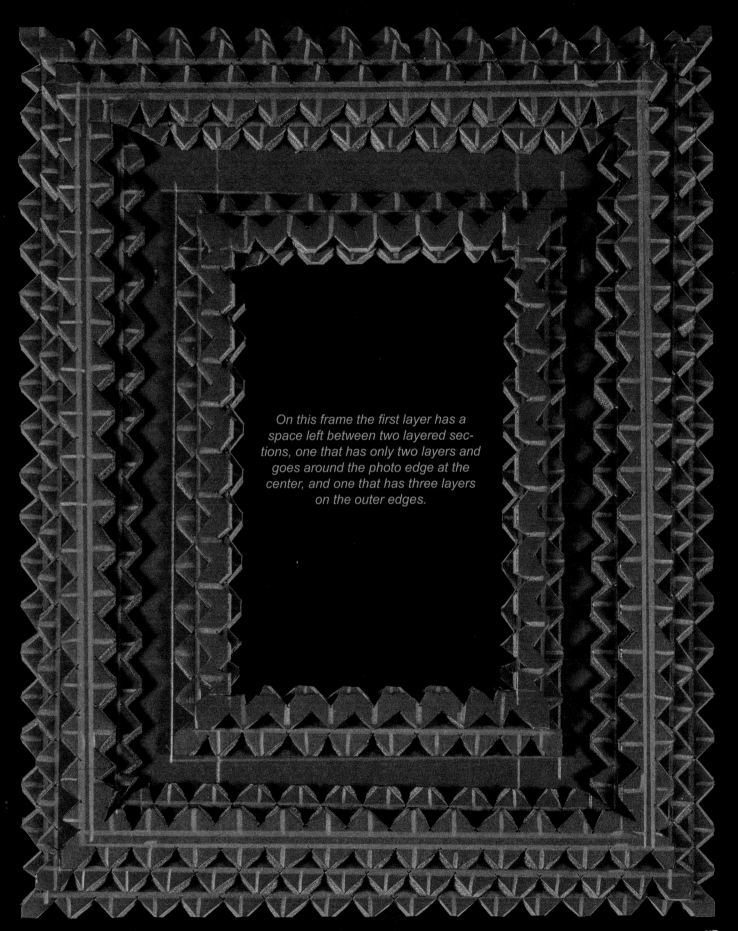

On this frame the first layer has a space left between two layered sections, one that has only two layers and goes around the photo edge at the center, and one that has three layers on the outer edges.

Oval Frame

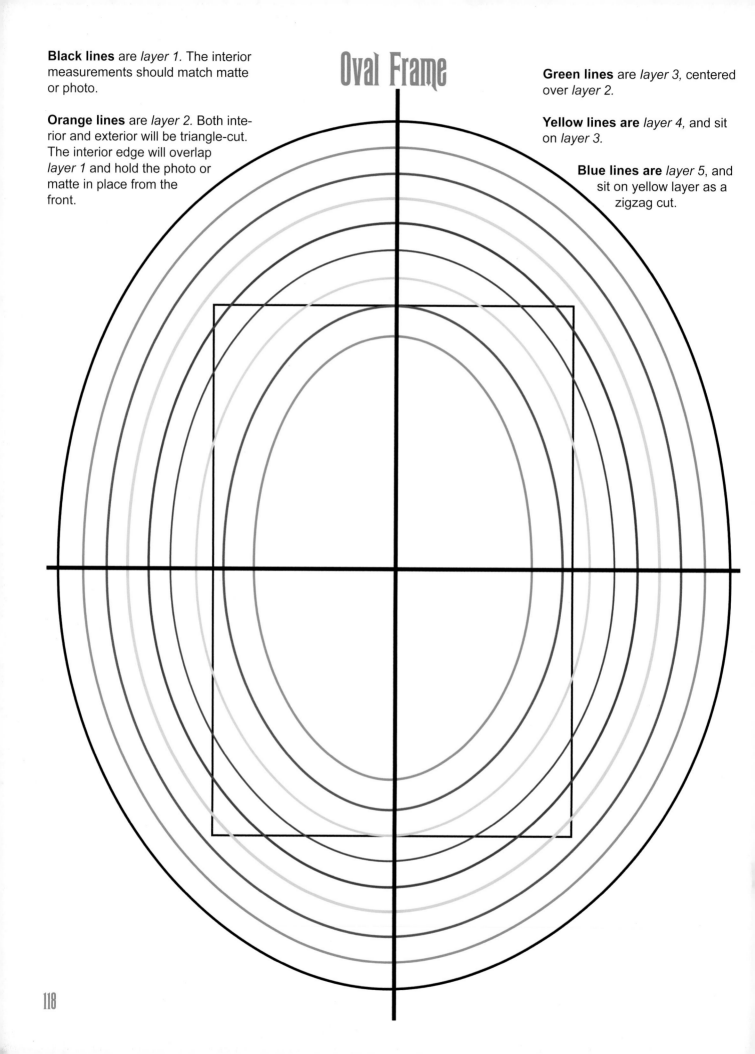

Black lines are *layer 1*. The interior measurements should match matte or photo.

Orange lines are *layer 2*. Both interior and exterior will be triangle-cut. The interior edge will overlap *layer 1* and hold the photo or matte in place from the front.

Green lines are *layer 3*, centered over *layer 2*.

Yellow lines are *layer 4*, and sit on *layer 3*.

Blue lines are *layer 5*, and sit on yellow layer as a zigzag cut.

This frame is a little trickier to mark out for the ½-inch marks on the curves but is totally worth the effort! The layers go from larger to smaller and would look good with or without a photo matte.

Black lines are *layer 1.* The interior measurements should match matte or photo.

Orange lines are *layer 2.* Both interior and exterior will be triangle-cut. The interior edge will overlap *layer 1* and hold the photo or matte in place from the front.

Green lines are *layer 3* and are created as individual pieces centered over *layer 2.*

Gray lines are *layer 4* and sit on *layer 3* as a zigzag cut.

This frame uses all connected corner layers and stacks from largest to smallest. The final layer is a zigzag cut. This frame lets even the smallest photo take center stage and get noticed.

Painting the Frames

1 Three craft paint colors were used to create the final look of the frames: *black, burnt umber, and red.* Together the layered colors make the foam core look like a nice antique cherry or rosewood.

2 First, using a chip brush and black paint, brush the entire frame, being sure to get every nook and corner. Let dry.

3 Next, mix a little of the red into the brown and stir. Dry brush over the black painted layer, leaving most of the nooks and corners in black. Don't be too precious with the painting. It should look like an antique painted wood in the end. Let dry.

4 Last, lightly paint with a straight red, using a brush, and wipe off most of the paint with a paper towel. You want a highlight of red. If you feel you have too much red, go back again with a little bit of black on those spots to tone it down. Let dry.

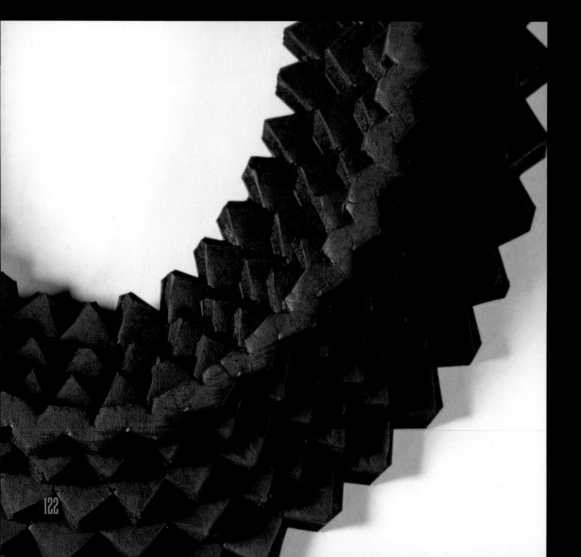

If too much red highlight is done, lightly brush the edges again with black to tone it down.

Some color samples showing edges highlighted with red

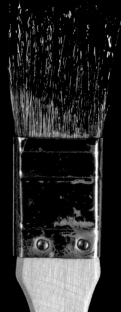

1

BLACK paint goes on first

2

BURNT UMBER with a touch of red paint goes on second

3

RED paint is used to highlight detail areas

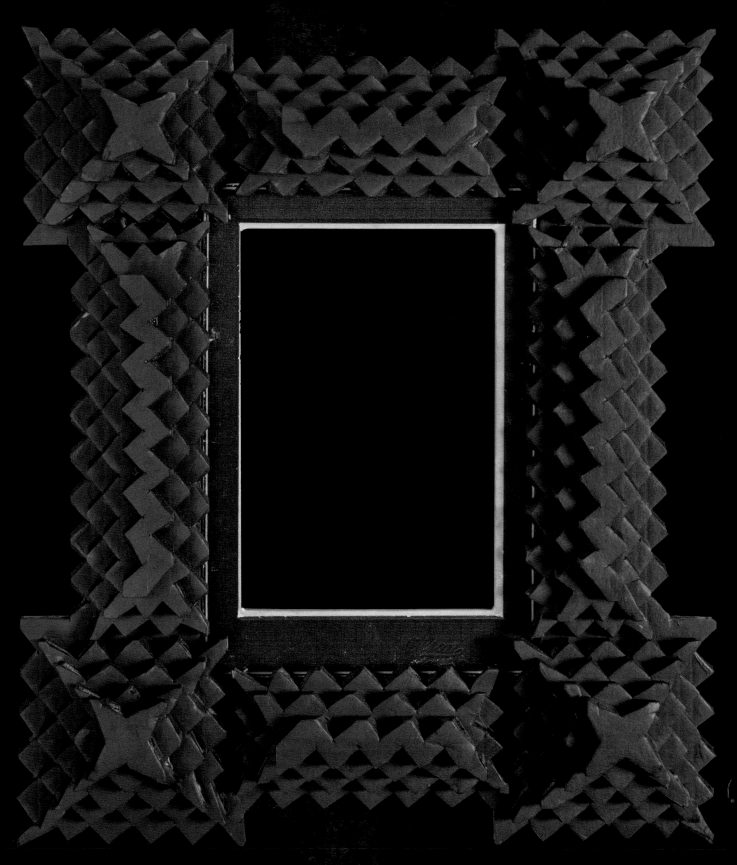

Final painted
Four -Corner Square Frame

*Final painted
Cat's-Ears Frame*

Final painted
Double Frame

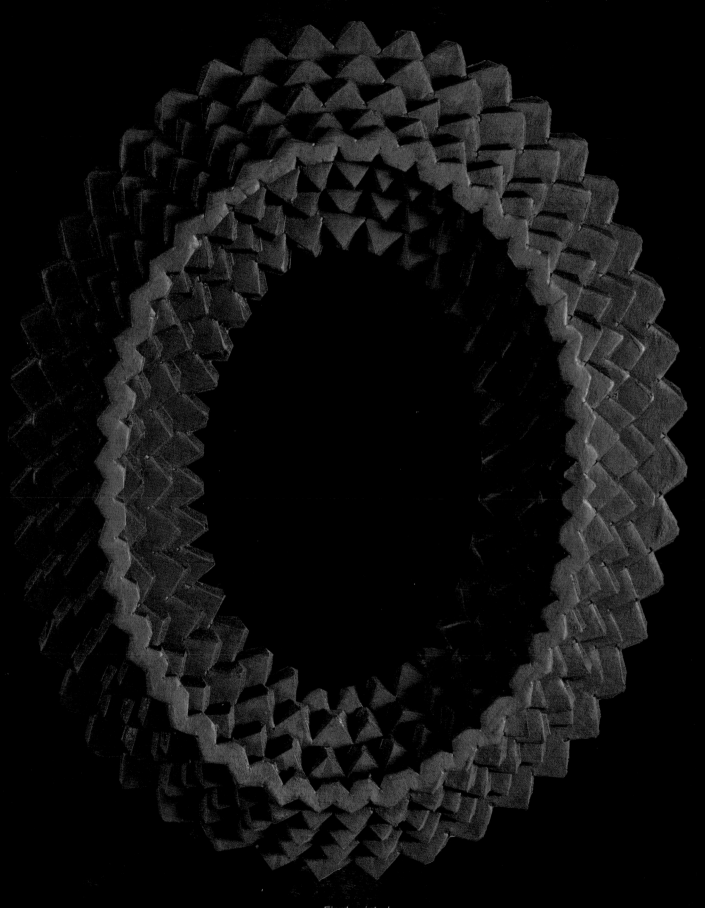

Final painted
Oval Frame

Back of the Frames

1 Place two Popsicle sticks on the back of the frame. If it gets too close to the edge, use the X-acto knife to trim some of the Popsicle stick as we did here. Then, cut out two small notches on each side of each stick. These notches will hold the wire that will hang the frame in the end.

2 Cut a piece of matte board or similar board as a flap to cover the photo area. Tape one side so it can be opened and a photo inserted.

3 Cut a thin wire double the length of the frame width. Twist one end of the wire tightly around each Popsicle stick. A loop can be created in the middle if you want the hanging material to show; otherwise, twist and bend it downward.

4 Glue the underside of both Popsicle sticks below the wire. Place glue side down on either side of the photo flap. Hold in place until the wood is secure and they don't slide out of position. Once the glue is dry, use black craft paint to cover the Popsicle sticks, including the stick sides.

5 Test the flap door. Once a photo has been added, secure the flap with a small piece of tape.

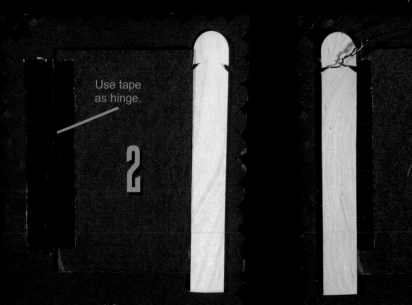

Any size Popsicle sticks may be used.

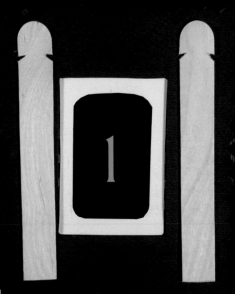

1

2

Use tape as hinge.

Final painted
Stack Frame

Connecting the
wire to the stick

Glue both Popsicle
sticks and add to
back of frame.

4

5

These frames look great in a variety of shapes and sizes
as a group and are a fun way to display
Halloween costume photos from years past.

10-Foot Bead Garland

YOU WILL NEED: Bags of pre-drilled wooden beads in a variety of sizes *(30mm, 20mm, 16mm, 14mm, and 12mm are good sizes to use);* wooden skewers; strong string; clear craft wax; craft paints in black, jack-o'-lantern orange, pumpkin orange, and harvest orange; paintbrush; Q-tips; old rag; coffee stirrer *(or kid's juice box straw);* Scotch tape; and some scraps of Styrofoam.

This custom, extra-long garland for the Halloween tree is made from painted wooden beads and string. The bags of pre-drilled beads were purchased on-line and can be ordered by size or as a mixed bag of various sizes. You can make one or more garlands, based on the number of beads purchased.

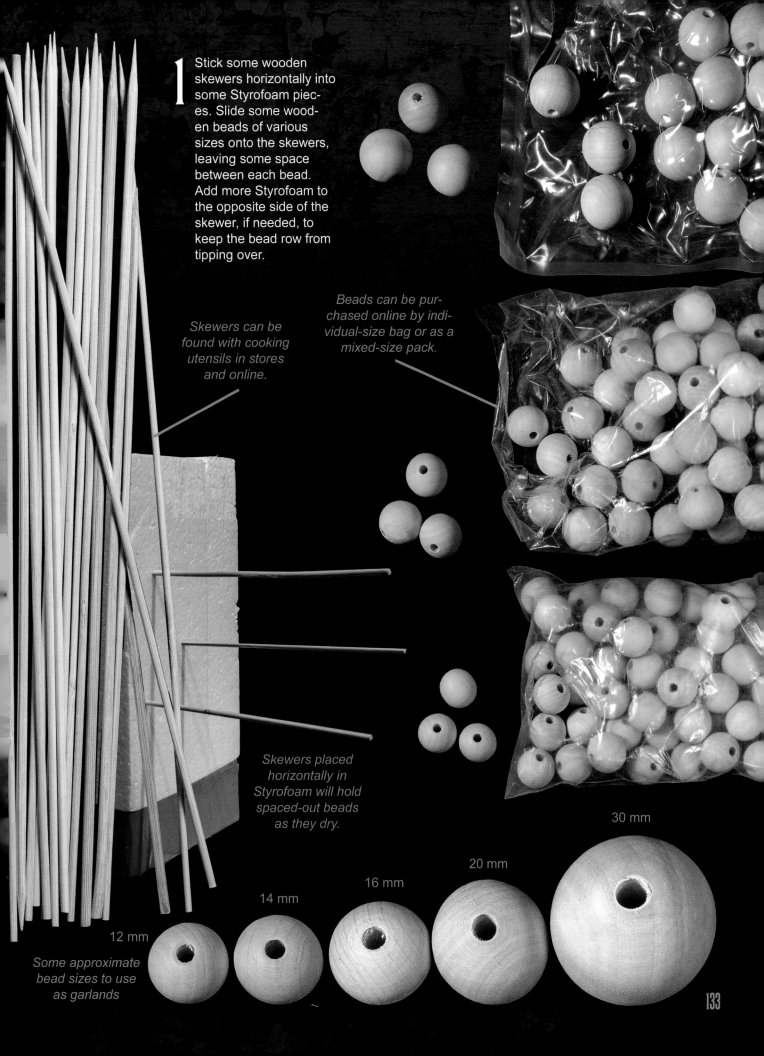

1 Stick some wooden skewers horizontally into some Styrofoam pieces. Slide some wooden beads of various sizes onto the skewers, leaving some space between each bead. Add more Styrofoam to the opposite side of the skewer, if needed, to keep the bead row from tipping over.

Skewers can be found with cooking utensils in stores and online.

Beads can be purchased online by individual-size bag or as a mixed-size pack.

Skewers placed horizontally in Styrofoam will hold spaced-out beads as they dry.

Some approximate bead sizes to use as garlands

12 mm

14 mm

16 mm

20 mm

30 mm

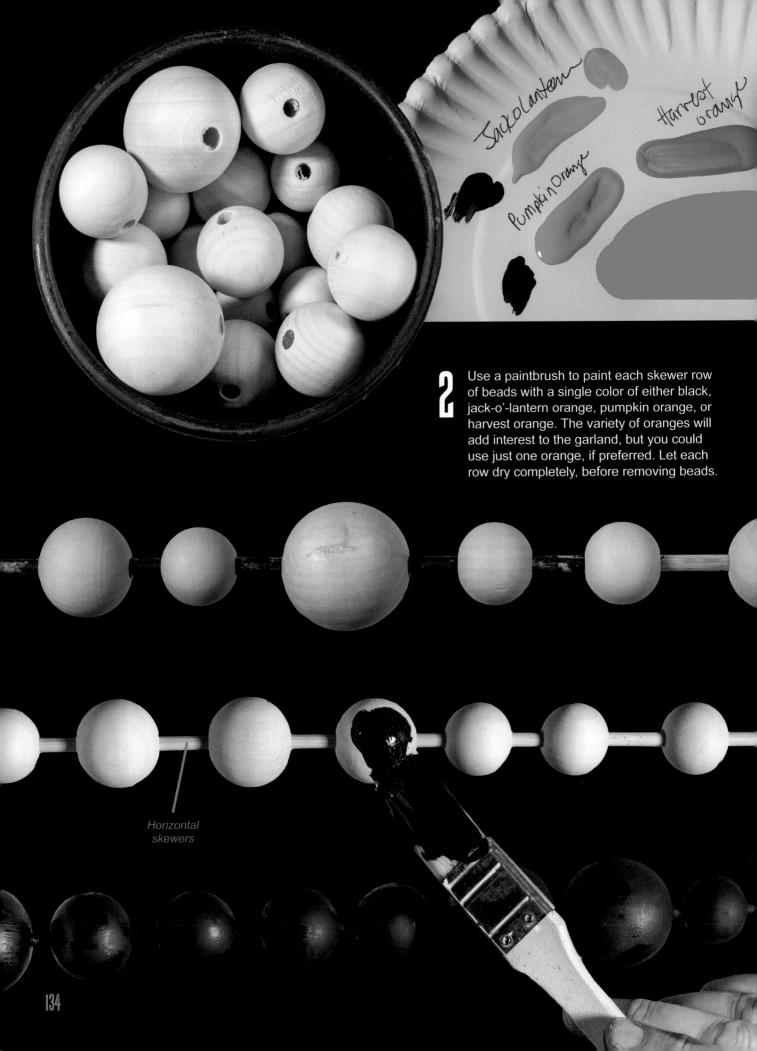

Jackolantern

Harvest orange

Pumpkin orange

2 Use a paintbrush to paint each skewer row of beads with a single color of either black, jack-o'-lantern orange, pumpkin orange, or harvest orange. The variety of oranges will add interest to the garland, but you could use just one orange, if preferred. Let each row dry completely, before removing beads.

Horizontal skewers

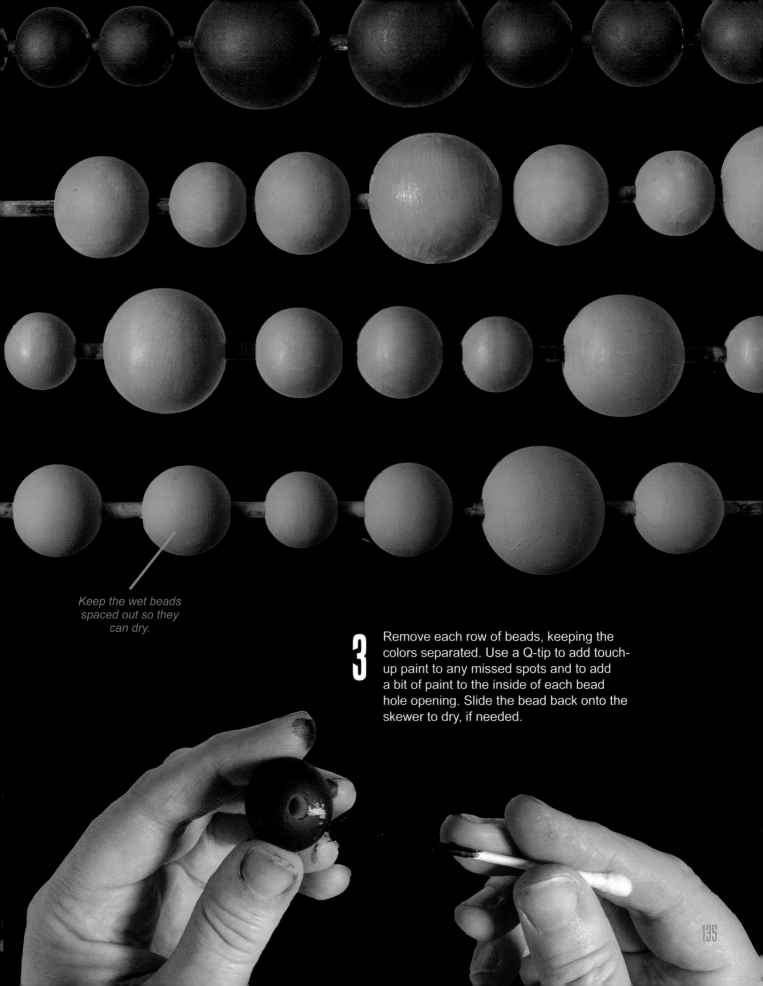

Keep the wet beads spaced out so they can dry.

3 Remove each row of beads, keeping the colors separated. Use a Q-tip to add touch-up paint to any missed spots and to add a bit of paint to the inside of each bead hole opening. Slide the bead back onto the skewer to dry, if needed.

KILZ
SEALING
clear wax

for use with CHALK STYLE PAI

SEAL & PROTECT FINISHED SURFAC

DANGER FLAMMABLE VAPOR.
COMBUSTIBLE MIXTURE. HARMFUL OR FATAL IF
SWALLOWED. See other cautions on back panel.

2.4 OZ. (68g)
NET WT.

4 Once all the beads are completely dry, use an old rag and clear wax to polish the surface of each bead. This will add a protective coating to the bead and protect it from damage.

TIP: If you still have leftover beads, create a second garland. We don't recommend going over a 10-foot length, since that many beads will get too heavy and could break the string.

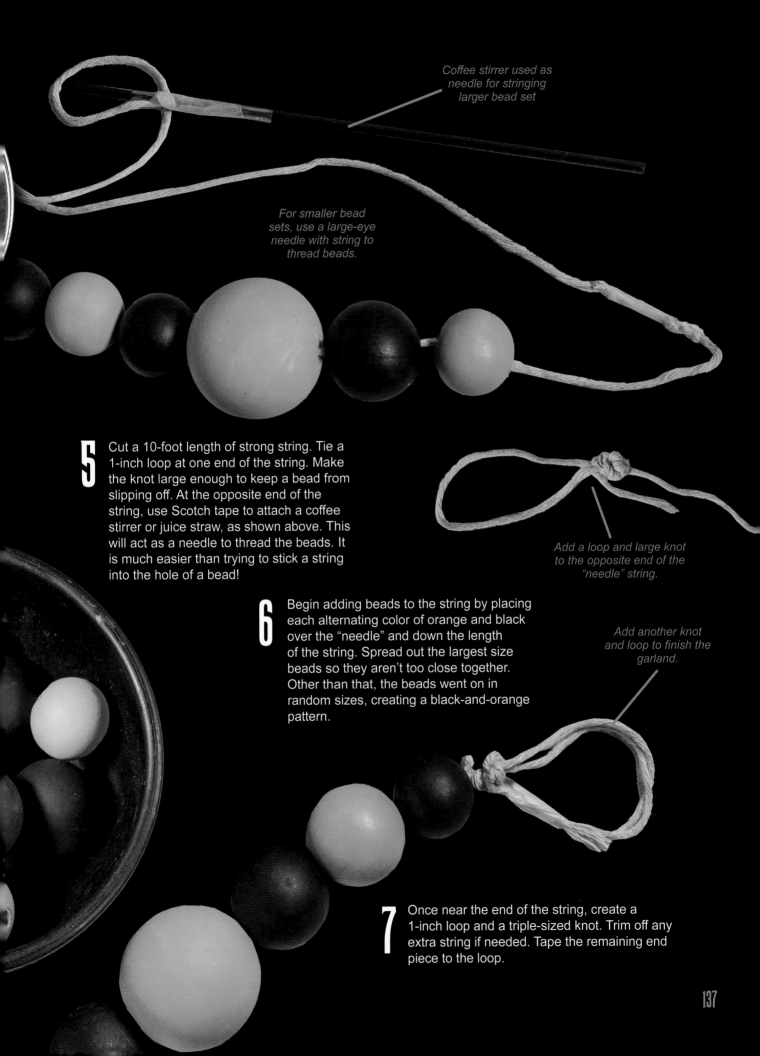

Coffee stirrer used as needle for stringing larger bead set

For smaller bead sets, use a large-eye needle with string to thread beads.

5 Cut a 10-foot length of strong string. Tie a 1-inch loop at one end of the string. Make the knot large enough to keep a bead from slipping off. At the opposite end of the string, use Scotch tape to attach a coffee stirrer or juice straw, as shown above. This will act as a needle to thread the beads. It is much easier than trying to stick a string into the hole of a bead!

Add a loop and large knot to the opposite end of the "needle" string.

6 Begin adding beads to the string by placing each alternating color of orange and black over the "needle" and down the length of the string. Spread out the largest size beads so they aren't too close together. Other than that, the beads went on in random sizes, creating a black-and-orange pattern.

Add another knot and loop to finish the garland.

7 Once near the end of the string, create a 1-inch loop and a triple-sized knot. Trim off any extra string if needed. Tape the remaining end piece to the loop.

When black cats prowl and pumpkins gleam.

May luck be yours on Halloween. ~Author Unknown

Trick-or-Treat Cones

Using Halloween Ribbon

YOU WILL NEED: variety of Halloween-themed ribbons and string, crepe paper in black and orange, scissors, low-heat glue gun and glue sticks, scanned or downloaded cone pattern, pencil, ruler, X-acto knife, thin wire, wire cutter *(needlenose pliers),* card stock or other heavy weight paper, Tacky Glue, Scotch tape, masking tape, cylindrical object approximately 1-inch diameter *(for rolling paper),* drill.

We have been collecting Halloween ribbons for years. The artwork, colors, and textures just make our spooky hearts beat faster. But one can make only so many bows! So, we came up with an easy project that really lets these ribbons take center stage. We can enjoy them year after year as candy treat containers that can be used as Halloween tree decorations, hung as colorful mantle décor, or as part of a table centerpiece.

You will need a variety of Halloween ribbons. Your Trick-or-Treat cones won't look exactly like ours, but you can take cues from how we selected different sizes and patterns and put them together.

So many incredible seasonal ribbons can be found each year. Start collecting them now!

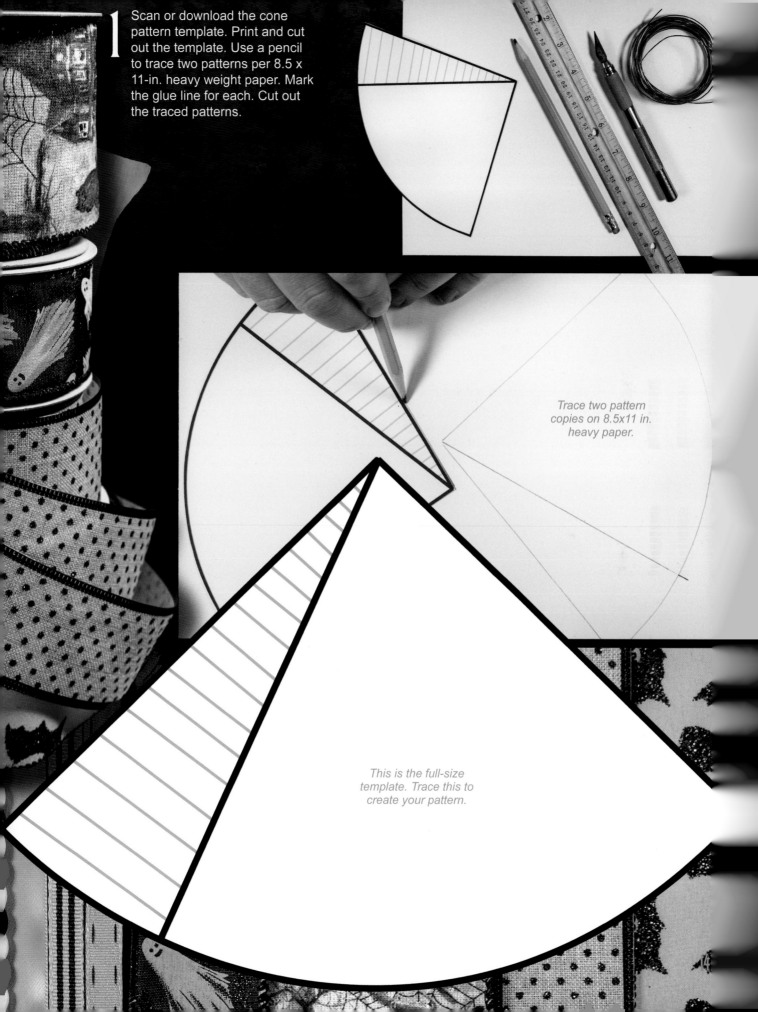

1 Scan or download the cone pattern template. Print and cut out the template. Use a pencil to trace two patterns per 8.5 x 11-in. heavy weight paper. Mark the glue line for each. Cut out the traced patterns.

Trace two pattern copies on 8.5x11 in. heavy paper.

This is the full-size template. Trace this to create your pattern.

A PVC pipe would also work for this step.

2
Use a cylindrical object, such as a faux candlestick or small PVC pipe, to roll each pattern from one of the straight edges. This will make gluing the cone much easier.

3
Add Tacky Glue to the glue section of the pattern. Match up the opposite straight edge to the inner glue edge as much as possible. Press together and add a piece of Scotch tape to top and bottom to hold in place.

4
Insert a pencil to the interior of the cone and use it to press the glue section from the inside.

5
Fold over two pieces of masking tape to opposite sides ½-inch from top edge of the cone. Use an X-acto knife to carefully add a small hole to the center of each masking taped area ¼-inch from top edge. The holes will be for the wire to be inserted.

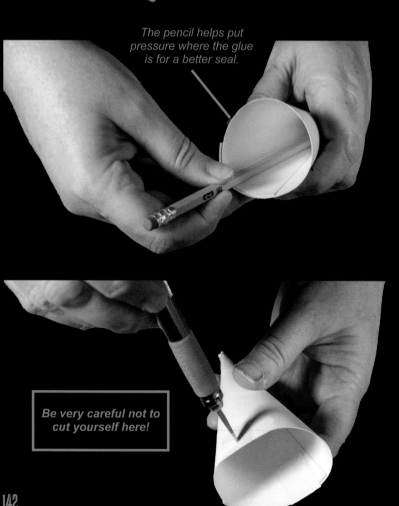

The pencil helps put pressure where the glue is for a better seal.

The tape gives extra strength to the cone, so it won't tear from the wire.

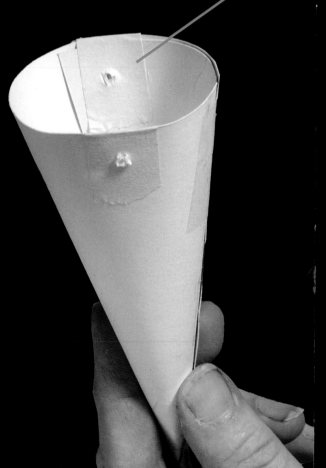

Be very careful not to cut yourself here!

Any color wire can be used for the treat cones.

Bend the wire ends.

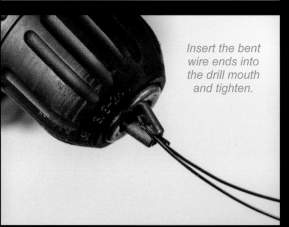

Insert the bent wire ends into the drill mouth and tighten.

With pliers holding the other wire end, slowly turn on the drill to twist the wire.

6 Cut a 20-inch piece of wire and bend in half. Use needlenose pliers to bend the loose ends of the wire over about ¼ inch from the ends.

7 Insert the bent ends of the wire into a drill bit slot and tighten. Hold the opposite folded wire end taut with the pliers.

8 Slowly turn on the drill so that it twists the wire evenly all the way down to the end. Don't overtwist or it will break the wire. Remove wire from drill bit. Use pliers to flatten the ends and cut twisted wire at the halfway point for two 5-inch pieces. This will be for two cones. Continue the wire process to make as many wire pieces as needed.

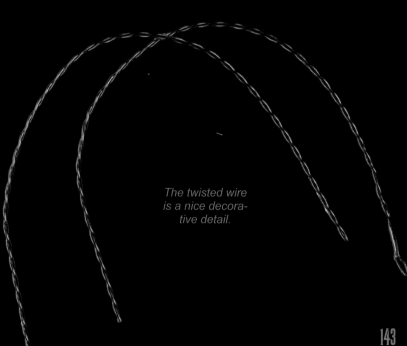

The twisted wire is a nice decorative detail.

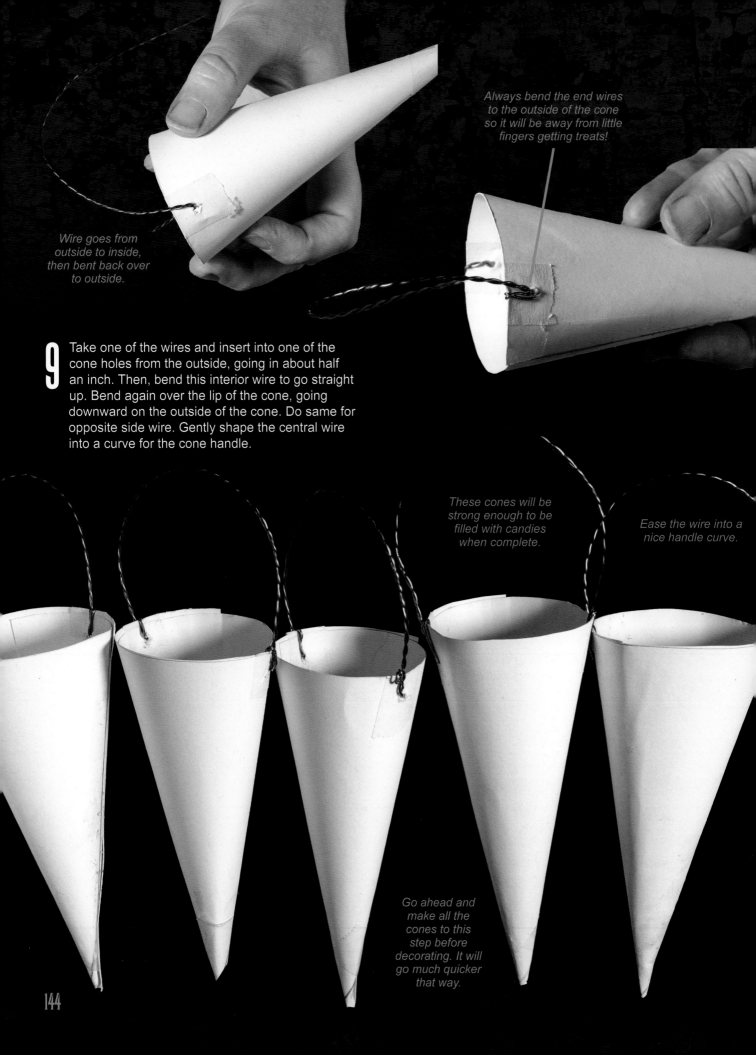

Always bend the end wires to the outside of the cone so it will be away from little fingers getting treats!

Wire goes from outside to inside, then bent back over to outside.

9 Take one of the wires and insert into one of the cone holes from the outside, going in about half an inch. Then, bend this interior wire to go straight up. Bend again over the lip of the cone, going downward on the outside of the cone. Do same for opposite side wire. Gently shape the central wire into a curve for the cone handle.

These cones will be strong enough to be filled with candies when complete.

Ease the wire into a nice handle curve.

Go ahead and make all the cones to this step before decorating. It will go much quicker that way.

10 Each cone will use either or both orange and black crepe paper to cover the tops of each cone. To prepare the crepe paper, cut approximately 12-inch lengths of each color. Use fingers to scrunch up into tight ¼-inch folds. Bunch the whole piece up and press tightly with fingers. Use scissors to cut this in half.

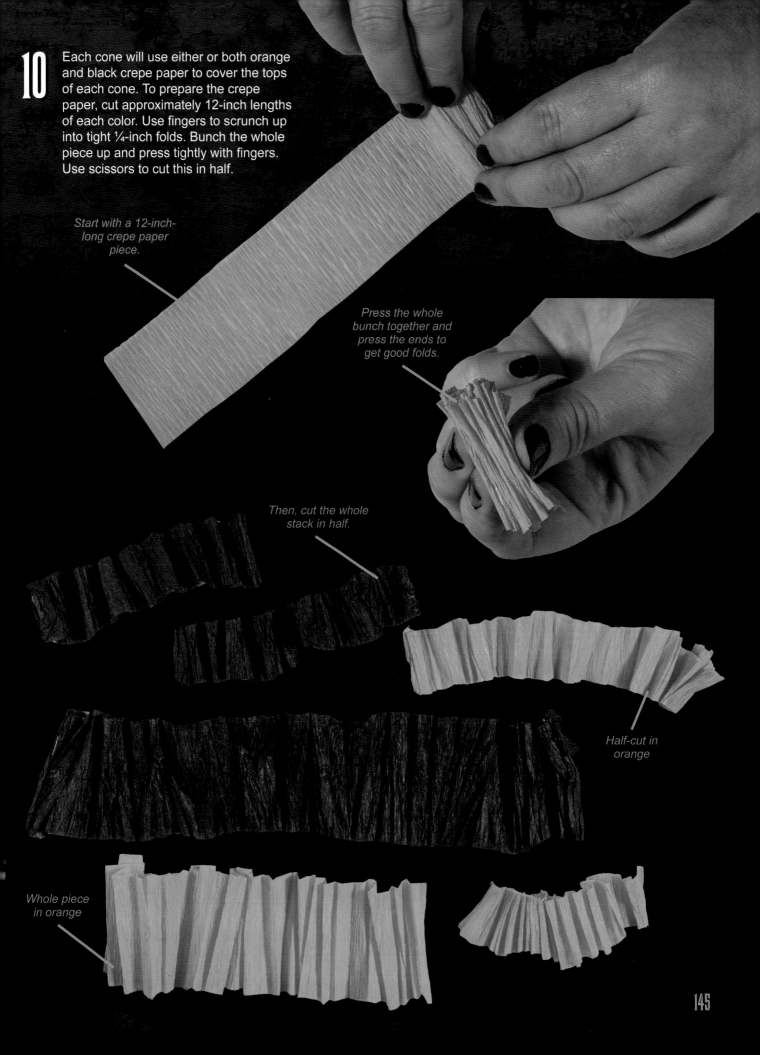

Start with a 12-inch-long crepe paper piece.

Press the whole bunch together and press the ends to get good folds.

Then, cut the whole stack in half.

Half-cut in orange

Whole piece in orange

Cone Design #1

1 Select ribbons that look good together, even if they have very different patterns. Here we stuck with a black-and-orange color scheme but used bats, ghosts, and polka dots. The two orange ribbons were slightly different tones, but that's all right; it still created an overall fun look.

2 The largest ribbon went on first, using Tacky Glue. Use a brush to spread the glue. Leave the edges unglued to be able to tuck other ribbons underneath the larger ones to finish off the edges better.

3 The second, polka dot ribbon, wrapped around to overlap the first ribbon and hot-glued in the center. We will cover up any spots that don't finish off neatly with more ribbons or decorative elements later.

Half bat ribbon and half polka dot ribbon covered most of the cone. Then, finish off the space with a third piece tucked under the first two ribbon edges.

4 Crinkle up a row of black and orange crepe paper into a stack and cut in half. These will be used around the top edges *(inside and out)* and on the cone end points. The crepe paper also covers up the inserted wire points.

Orange was hot-glued to the inside cone rim, and black was glued to outside cone rim and over wires.

Low-temp hot glue or Tacky Glue can be used for attaching ribbons and crepe paper pieces to cones. Hot glue sticks faster, whereas Tacky Glue has a little more stick time.

Smaller ribbons are a great thing to hide any problem areas of the design.

5 Once the surface of the cone is complete, add any extra embellishments needed to complete the treat cone. Here we layer-stacked one end of a ribbon. The folds were hot-glued in place. The ribbon then covered any spots with an unfinished edge or to hide any spots we didn't like.

Cut the thin ribbon end on an angle and hot-glue a few decorative folds for interest.

Aleene's ORIGINAL

ORIGINAL
TACKY GLUE

America's Favorite
CRAFT GLUE

Premium All-Purpose Adhesive
Tout Usage de Première Qualité
vo Multiuso de Calidad Premium

FL OZ (473 mL)

Larger design elements on ribbons can be cut out and used as decorative embellishments.

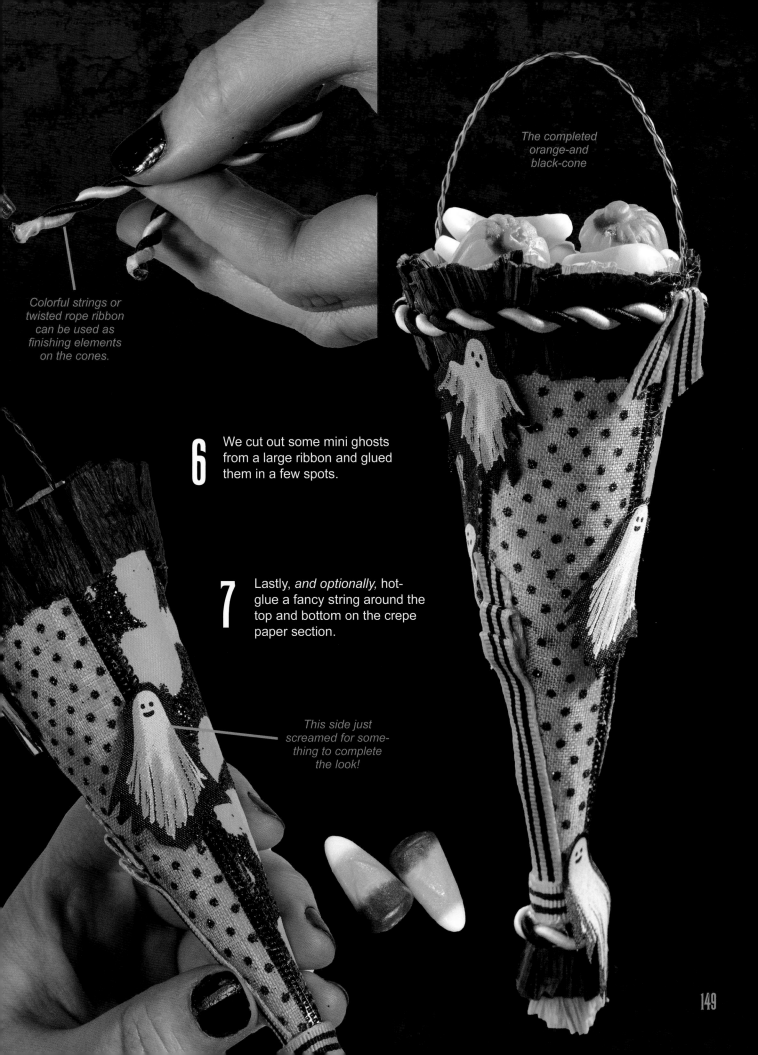

Colorful strings or twisted rope ribbon can be used as finishing elements on the cones.

6 We cut out some mini ghosts from a large ribbon and glued them in a few spots.

7 Lastly, *and optionally,* hot-glue a fancy string around the top and bottom on the crepe paper section.

This side just screamed for something to complete the look!

The completed orange-and-black-cone

This cone used a large orange-and-black ribbon to start off the design. The same ribbon was used to completely cover the cone base.

Next, a thin dotted ribbon was crisscrossed around the cone over the first ribbon.

Add the black and orange crepe paper around the top cone rim and bottom cone point.

Top-to-bottom ribbon technique. Spread the Tacky Glue with a brush, leaving the ribbon edges unglued.

Trim the ribbons along the top of the cone edge.

Use low-temp hot glue to add the crepe paper edging. Glue about 1 inch, then press the paper on, then continue on the next inch.

The final ribbon will tuck under the first ribbon edges. The edges can then be Tacky Glued or hot-glued.

Glue

Glue inside loop
behind center.

These bows aren't
tied; they are glued
in the center.

4 Three small ribbon bows were created.
To create the bow, first, cross two ends
of ribbon and glue in place. Next, glue
the back loop to the underside of the
two tails. Two of these ribbons were
placed on opposite sides near the top
and one near the bottom.

Final #2
treat cone

The crisscrossed
polka dot ribs is just
the right amount of
fancy for this treat
cone!

Add one more
tiny polka dot rib-
bon to finish off
at the cone tip.

These bows have
a flatter surface
to attach with,
using hot glue.

1 This large ribbon had a bit of glitter sparkle on a haunted house with cobweb scene. We paired it with some ghost ribbon, lining up the wired edges for a nice, finished edge.

2 Tuck any ends under the edge of the larger ribbon with a tiny amount of hot glue.

3 We also used some black-and-orange-striped ribbon to create the cone endpiece and a fancy fringe with a bow in the center.

This wide ribbon has a wired-edge detail.

This technique lines up the wired-edge ribbons side by side where possible.

Hot-glue the crepe paper in two offset rows in double black and double orange.

This little flower detail is a rolled-up ribbon that has been cut into fringe on one end.

A few wired thin-cut ribbon pieces clustered together form a unique endpiece for the final cone design.

Cone Design #4

1 A large ribbon with glitter bats on orange background was used as the main wrap on this treat cone.

The striped ribbon was a medium-size wire-edged ribbon that was glued on at an angle in three rows.

2 The second ribbon was a black-and-white stripe and was wrapped around, edge-to-edge, on half of the cone.

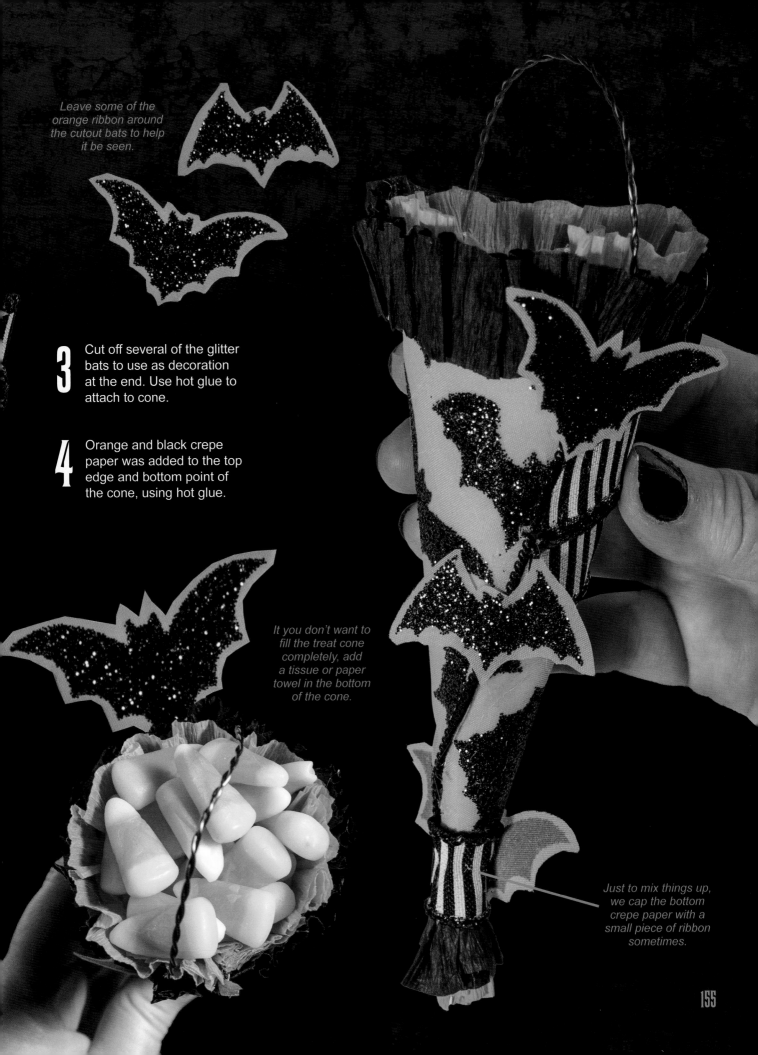

Leave some of the orange ribbon around the cutout bats to help it be seen.

3 Cut off several of the glitter bats to use as decoration at the end. Use hot glue to attach to cone.

4 Orange and black crepe paper was added to the top edge and bottom point of the cone, using hot glue.

It you don't want to fill the treat cone completely, add a tissue or paper towel in the bottom of the cone.

Just to mix things up, we cap the bottom crepe paper with a small piece of ribbon sometimes.

1 The large haunted house ribbon was paired with the black-and-white striped thinner ribbon and a smaller piece of ghost ribbon.

Making all these Hallow-een treat cones secretly inspires Christmas ribbon versions too.

We have stocked up or orange and black crepe paper, so we can work with it all year long.

2 After the black and orange crepe paper was added to the top edge and bottom point, a final black-and-white twisted string was added to the crepe paper.

The twisted black-and-white string was wrapped around the cone end over the crepe paper and hot-glued in place.

Cone Design #6

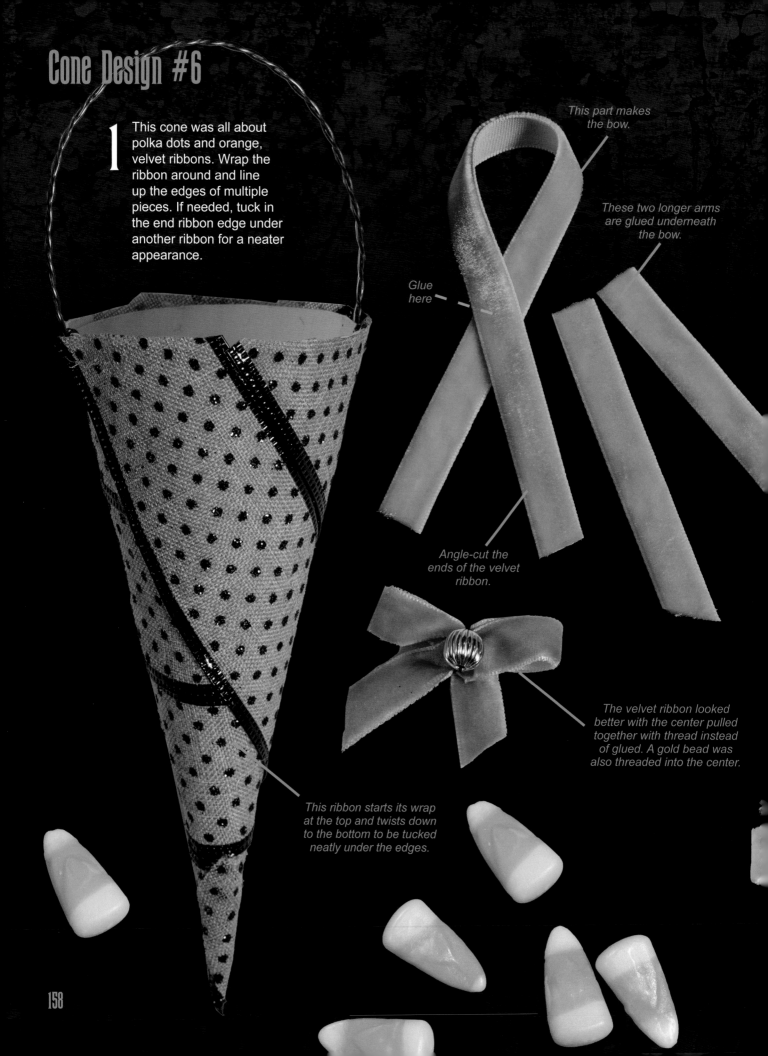

1 This cone was all about polka dots and orange, velvet ribbons. Wrap the ribbon around and line up the edges of multiple pieces. If needed, tuck in the end ribbon edge under another ribbon for a neater appearance.

This part makes the bow.

These two longer arms are glued underneath the bow.

Glue here

Angle-cut the ends of the velvet ribbon.

The velvet ribbon looked better with the center pulled together with thread instead of glued. A gold bead was also threaded into the center.

This ribbon starts its wrap at the top and twists down to the bottom to be tucked neatly under the edges.

2 To make the velvet bow, cut an 8-inch length of ribbon, cross two ends, and add a drop of glue to hold where they cross. Bring the back loop center underneath the cross point and glue it in place on the back. Use sewing thread to tighten the bow center. Loop thread around the bow and through the gold bead and tie in back.

3 Make two velvet bows with two extra-long arm ribbon pieces. Hot-glue bow and arms on opposing sides near top, as shown on right.

This finished cone is the fancy lady treat cone with orange velvet, polka dots, and black crepe.

These spooky ghosts are flying everywhere this Halloween!

This satin ribbon is wired, so it was folded up in an interesting way and hot-glued into place at the end.

1 This cone was covered completely in a wide width ghost ribbon.

2 Cut a couple of the cute ghosts out of the ribbon, leaving a small amount of border.

3 Add orange crepe paper to top edge and bottom point of cone. Hot glue to attach.

4 Using a small, wired ribbon, cut two pieces, about 3-inches long, and crinkle up the ends to look as if they are flowing. Angle the top ends to meet, and glue together with hot glue.

5 Glue one of the cutout ghosts to the top of the ribbons and glue the whole piece to the cone. Make one for each side.

Three layers of orange crepe, slightly offset, went around the outside rim, with one more layer on the inside.

Two cutout ghost's top each of the decorative wires and are attached with a drop of hot glue.

These sugar candies might not get eaten, since they are hung on the tree, but they add to the overall festive feel.

161

Cone Design #8

Three layers of offset black crepe paper on the outer cone rim, with one more layer for the inner rim.

Create six rows of wire-edged ribbon and glue edge to edge until you reach the end.

162

1 Using all black-and-white striped ribbon, glue top edge at an angle to the cone. Continue to glue as the ribbon is twisted all the way down to the bottom tip of the cone.

2 Line the next ribbon piece to the previous ribbon border at the top and follow around, matching the border edges. Glue as you wrap. Continue until the entire cone is covered.

3 Add three layers of black crepe paper to top and one layer to inner cone rim. Then, wrap several more layers around bottom tip and glue.

4 Finish off the cone by gluing a black-and-white twisted string over the crepe paper cone tip.

This lovely treat cone is inspired by Katrina Van Tassel's dress from the movie Sleepy Hollow.

Halloween Tree Ornaments

YOU WILL NEED: Several mini plastic skulls *(same used in the Miniature Ghosts on pages 20–33);* wooden skewers; gold and black craft paint; drill with large screw *(for making holes);* thin, decorative wire; large 1-inch buttons *(one for each skull);* hot-glue gun with glue sticks; needlenose pliers; orange crepe paper; paintbrush; scrap of Styrofoam or cardboard box.

This Halloween tree ornament project is scary simple to make. Once again, a bag of mini skulls comes in handy, and you can fill out that Halloween tree in no time with these custom ornaments. Paint the skulls in a color scheme that matches your theme. They could be metallic *(as we have done here),* black and orange, purple, or white.

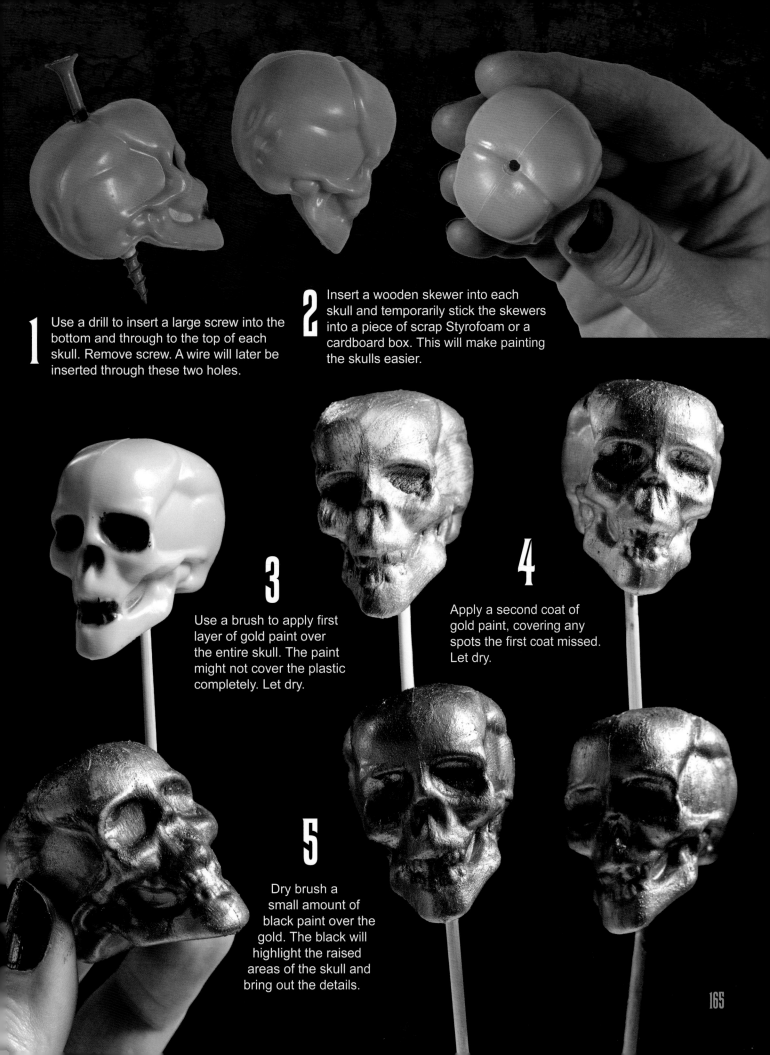

1 Use a drill to insert a large screw into the bottom and through to the top of each skull. Remove screw. A wire will later be inserted through these two holes.

2 Insert a wooden skewer into each skull and temporarily stick the skewers into a piece of scrap Styrofoam or a cardboard box. This will make painting the skulls easier.

3 Use a brush to apply first layer of gold paint over the entire skull. The paint might not cover the plastic completely. Let dry.

4 Apply a second coat of gold paint, covering any spots the first coat missed. Let dry.

5 Dry brush a small amount of black paint over the gold. The black will highlight the raised areas of the skull and bring out the details.

165

Any color wire can be used. If you don't have a button, you can use a 1-inch washer.

Bend ends over ¼ inch.

Hot-glue where the wire meets the button on top, while holding the wire straight up until glue is cool.

6 Cut a 10-inch piece of decorative wire. Fold it in half.

7 Insert the two wire ends into two opposing holes of a large 1-inch button. Bend the two wire ends over about a quarter inch.

Hot-glue where the wire meets the button on the bottom.

8 Use a handheld drill with the drill bit removed. Insert the bent wire ends into the drill bit and tighten. Hold the button firmly, with wire level to the drill bit. Very slowly turn on the drill and let the wire twist together until it gets close to the button. Remove the wire from the drill. Use wire cutters to clip off the bent ends of the wires.

9 With the button sitting on a flat surface, hold the wire straight up from the button. Add a small amount of hot glue to the wire where it meets the button. Once the glue is firm, turn button to other side and add a small amount of glue to that side. Let cool. Set aside.

Use needlenose pliers to cut off the bent wire ends.

The skull should fit easily over the wire. Test-fit to be sure it fits.

Make a lot of the half-size orange crepe (or black if you prefer).

10 Cut a 10-inch piece of orange crepe paper. Lay it on a flat surface and use fingers to pinch up the entire length. Cut the bunch in half. Do this until you have a nice little pile.

11 Use low-temperature hot glue on the wire side of the button and begin attaching one of the half strands of crepe paper. Turn and glue all the way around the button with several layers of crepe paper.

Keep building bulk until you get a thick ruffle for the base of the skull.

12 Stick the wire into a piece of scrap Styrofoam or a cardboard box so that you can work on the bottom of the button. Do the same hot glue and crepe paper to this side for several layers.

Once the stack is complete, use your fingers to press in and crunch up the layers to separate.

13 To finish the bottom side, on the last layer turn and glue, make it a smaller spiral. Glue the endpiece of crepe paper so the button is no longer visible.

Bend the wire horizontally against the top of the skull to keep it in place.

14 The crepe paper collar can be as thin or thick as you desire. Once collar is done, insert a painted skull head onto the wire and down over the crepe paper.

15 Bend the wire where it meets the back of skull, so that it holds it in place. Then zigzag bend the rest of the wire upward, with the wire end forming a downward curve as shown. This will be the ornament hook to hang it on a tree.

Top of wire is bent over to form the hanging hook.

Get creative with the wire. Try twisting it into a spiral around a pencil for a different look.

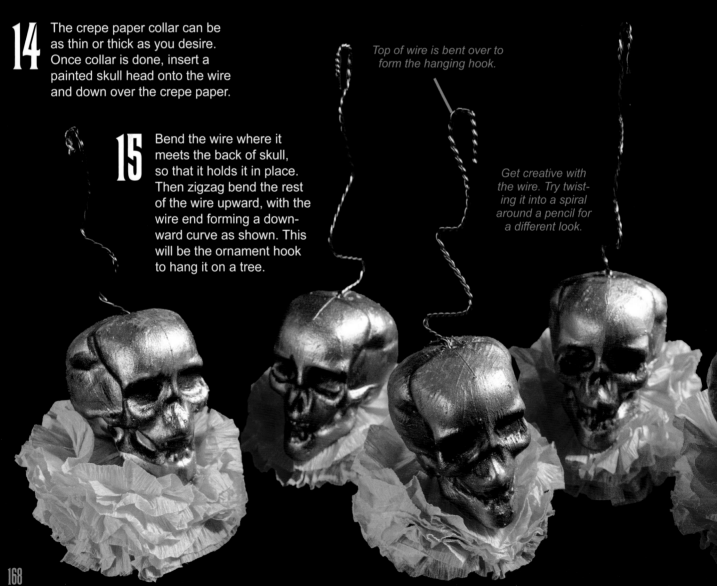

*Custom-made
non-breakable
ornaments for the
Halloween tree!*

Decorating

for a Handmade Halloween

Whether your gathering is just for the kids or a full-blown All Hallows Eve extravaganza, decorating for the season should inspire and delight all the souls, both in body and *spirit form*. Fall has arrived and, with it, the time to bring out all these handcrafted projects the family has made and decorate for Halloween!

1 Decorating Tip Deck the halls with orange and black! Christmas might rule with red and green, but the Halloween banner flies high with orange and black. So, start the season off right with a change of colors . . . swap out the dishtowels and soaps. Then move on to a table centerpiece of pumpkins and dark-inspired flowers. Light the pumpkin-scented candles and brew up some spiced coffee or cocoa.

The Decorating Plan

1 ROOM TO THEME   Decide which room or rooms will be decorated. Will there be a theme this year or will it just be a free-for-all pull out the holiday bins and see what happens? You don't always have to decorate every square inch of the house. If this year has been difficult, simplify the decorating to just a few places, such as porch and dining area. Or, if you just want to lie back and watch all your favorite holiday movies, then turn the *living* room . . . into *a dead room.*

2 HANDY HANGERS   Make sure you have plenty of tape, stick-on hooks, string, scissors, and batteries before decorating. Nothing is more frustrating than having to stop everything and run to the store for the ceiling hooks you forgot before you can decorate.

3 DÉCOR LEVELS   Keep it stress-free. If you have young kids or lots of pets, keep the delicate decorating up high and out of reach of curious hands and paws. Down low can be pillows, blankets, battery-operated candles, and fun Halloween rugs.

4 SET THE VIBE YouTube has loads of music channels for all eras of Halloween music. You can listen to classic Halloween tunes from the 1920s to the 1990s. It's a fun way to decorate.

2 Decorating Tip Keep your decorations organized by color or branded themes based on a favorite movie or book. This way, you can mix it up year after year, without having to pull out and sort through every container. For example, décor items in all orange and black, gothic-glam, witches, or ghosts could be divided up by color or theme. *Hocus Pocus, Beetlejuice, Haunted Mansion*, and *Harry Potter*–branded items would each have their own container. Be sure to label each container!

3 Decorating Tip

String the mantle or under-neath shelves with multiple garlands in orange and black. The wooden letters that say "HAPPY HALLOWEEN" were purchased. The black letters didn't show up on the dark background. Out came the orange paint . . . just to paint the edges. Don't be afraid to alter store-bought items.

4 Decorating Tip Lighting the indoor decorations should create a festive mood, be safe, and tie in with the Halloween décor. We set up a lot of battery-operated candles that turn on and off with a remote control. To make them more interesting, we add a few hot-glue drips on the candle sides, but we also vary the candle heights. From candelabras to individual candleholders, place some high and some lower around the room. Place some LED color ambient lights that can sit behind the handmade props and backlight with a selected color. Blue, green, red, and yellow are good color options. Try out different colors to see what looks the best. Make sure to test how hot the lights get. Some LED lights do get warm. If they do, make sure they are not touching any paper or fabric or any surface that might be affected.

5 Decorating Tip Have a bead-stringing spooky pajama party! Make sure there is plenty of popcorn and candy corn to fuel the festivities . . . or to use as more garland-making materials.

6 Decorating Tip

Why not make a photographic album or scrapbook with a Halloween-only rule? Have everyone help decorate the covers with leftover costume scraps. Then, each person can contribute their favorite photos of making costumes, painting faces, standing in line at a haunted attraction, carving pumpkins, watching scary movies, party recipes, pet costumes, completed decorating projects, Halloween hauls, and anything else related to the spooky season!

179

7 Decorating Tip The Halloween tree has been steadily growing in popularity. If you don't want to go big, find a thin, tall tree *(or two!)* and use plastic jack-o'-lanterns as the base and tree topper. Weight the base with bricks or bags of sand so it doesn't topple over. The plastic jack-o'-lanterns also look great with string lights inside and cast an orange glow over the treat-filled ornaments. Circle the tree with the same bead garlands and crepe paper strands. What kid *(or adult)* wouldn't want to come down on Halloween morning to discover pre-filled candy buckets beneath the Halloween tree?

8 Decorating Tip A time to reflect on seasons past. Make a special area to display past Halloweens in your custom Halloween frames. Whether it is trips to the farm to gather pumpkins or costume themes through the years . . . remembering the fun ways the family enjoyed past seasons and time together is always a positive thing and will inspire future Halloween ideas.

9 Decorating Tip Bring on the crepe paper! The more you make, the more fun you will have finding ways to use it. When the season is over, pack it up and store for year-after-year use.

HAPPY HALLOWEEN

The Feast of Treats

No baking required. Everything at this impromptu party was store-bought but taken up a few creative notches. The mini cupcakes were topped with ghosts. The plain popcorn balls were drizzled with blood-red sugar and sprinkled with candy corn. The candy and cookies were displayed on tiered cupcake holders and spooky dishes. The kid's eyes went wide when they came in and saw this *Feast of Treats* table laid out!

A few ideas for shopping are colorful cupcakes, cookies, candy, popcorn balls, fall-flavored cakes, apple ciders, fizzy sodas with a touch of orange or green, pumpkin-spiced coffee for the adults, pumpkin-spiced cocoa for the kids, chocolate-covered pretzel sticks, caramel apples, cotton candy, candied nuts, and dried fruits . . . just to name a few delectable treats that can be found around the holiday season.

10 Decorating Tip Keep the colors in the shades of Halloween *(orange, black, green, and yellow)*, and it will all look planned out and theme coordinated. Most of the platters and plates were dark and really allowed those seasonal colors to shine through. The table was covered with leftover panels of distressed cheesecloth. The irregular edges were allowed to drape over the sides, and a few small pieces of tape held the fabric to the table, keeping everything in place.

11 Decorating Tip Create a kid's drink bar with Halloween drink dispenser in both green and orange colors. Orange-colored drinks for kids include Orange Sunkist, orange-flavored Kool-Aid, and orange Tang. Green Fanta is a green-colored soda that tastes like candy apples. Other green drinks include Green River *(lime & lemon flavors)* soda, lemon-lime or green apple Kool-Aid, and Hawaiian Punch Green Berry. Have a stack of fun Halloween cups and straws, and you have a complete kid's drink bar.

190

12 Decorating Tip Make sure to have plenty of fun Halloween-shaped glasses or headbands for easy decorating attire to go with those Halloween pajamas. This keeps the mood fun and provides tons of photographic moments. Make sure to take photos for all those project frames you made!

13 Decorating Tip

If Trick or Treating is a no-go this year . . . why not let the kids go on a candy hunt? Instead of looking for Easter eggs . . . the hunt will be on for hidden Halloween candy! *Let the jack-o'-lanterns be filled!*

Thank You!

The Mitchell Family would like to deeply thank Schiffer Publishing, the editors, and marketing department for all their hard work in seeing this new project through to the completed product. We couldn't have done it without you. We would also like to thank all those who take the time to review our work, pass the word around, and support our small business in the purchase of this book. The Mitchell Family is continuing to inspire and create in all things Halloween. *Long may we all haunt!*

Be sure to check out our other books

Best of How to Haunt Your House, Volumes 1 & 2 sold in bookstores, online retailers, or our website: **www.howtohauntyourhouse.com.**

You can also check us out on social media:
https://www.pinterest.com/howtohaunt
https://www.facebook.com/howtohaunt/
https://www.youtube.com/howtohaunt
https://www.instagram.com/howtohaunt/

Credits

Font credits: *Ravenscroft font* was originally conceived and drawn by Tim McKenny, then refined and developed by Justin Callaghan.
www.micheyavenue.com

Photography by Shawn and Lynne Mitchell. All projects and artwork in this book were made and tested by the Mitchell Family.

Index